Japanese Religious Attitudes

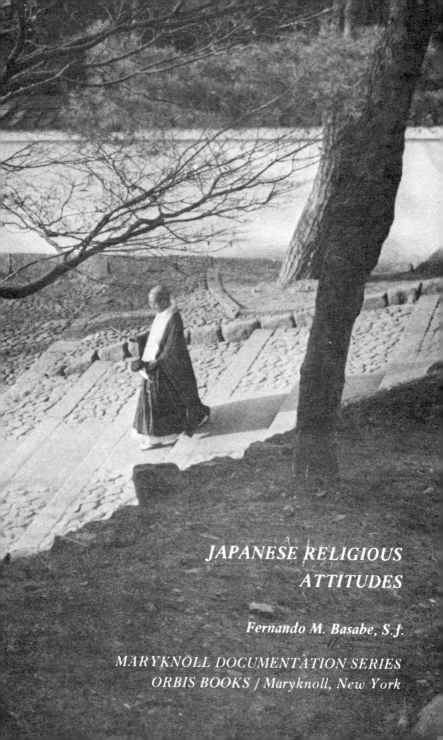

JAPANESE RELIGIOUS ATTITUDES

Fernando M. Basabe, S.J.

MARYKNOLL DOCUMENTATION SERIES
ORBIS BOOKS / Maryknoll, New York

This book originally appeared as *Religious Attitudes,* Jesuit Sociological Survey: Japan, Report No. 7. Privately published in Tokyo, 1968. This is a brief summary of two surveys on the religious attitudes of Japanese youth and the Japanese man in the street. The research was carried out by a group of professors of Sophia University, Tokyo—S. Anzai; F. Lanzaco, S.J.; A. M. Nebreda, S.J.; and F. M. Basabe, S.J.—during the years 1966-1968. Reports on these surveys were published in Tokyo in *Monumenta Nipponica* in two articles, both written by Father Basabe: "Japanese Youth Confronts Religion" (1967) and "Religious Attitudes of Japanese Men" (1969).

Copyright © 1972, Orbis Books,
Maryknoll, Communications, Maryknoll N.Y. 10545
Library of Congress Catalog Card Number: 70 — 188666

Design by La Liberté & Rayner
Manufactured in the United States of America

CONTENTS

PREFACE

This book was originally one of eleven reports on sociological surveys of the principal institutions of Japanese society. The surveys were made in accord with the desire of Pedro Arrupe, superior general of the Society of Jesus, to have surveys on the basic structures of contemporary society in each country so that the Society's apostolic work could be more effectively adapted to the concrete conditions of today's world. The study of these structures is the first part of a general survey of the Society itself, which was launched by Father Arrupe on December 9, 1965.

My colleagues in the underlying research and subsequent analyses recognize that this report on the religious attitudes of Japanese youth and the Japanese man in the street is by no means conclusive. We hope it will engender further studies and so be constantly revised and brought up to date.

A word of thanks is due to Rev. M. Suarez and Mr. V. Bona, who worked very zealously in the preparation of the materials for publications.

F.M.B.

*Student: "Insofar as you come to believe in religion,
you entangle yourself in a prearranged system of thought."*

Student: "I feel envious of a man who can really believe from his heart in a religion, and I myself would like to come to such a state."

INTRODUCTION
THE RELIGIOUS SITUATION IN JAPAN

From the very beginning of our research we were fully aware of the tremendous difficulties posed by an analysis of the Japanese religious mentality. The Japanese religious world appears to the eyes of the researcher as an unfathomable mystery. All Japanese religion scholars speak of the difficulties involved in attempting an analysis of the religious aspects of present-day Japan, where a secular Buddhistic and Shintoistic tradition persists; where the authentic religious faith is in a state of acute crisis; where a majority of the young adults do not profess to have any religious beliefs; and where, nevertheless, there exists a blossoming of new religions and sects which are but an amalgam of conflicting beliefs from all of the world's principal religions—a kind of "museum of all the religions that today exist in the world," according to Kishimoto Hideo.

Recently the Ministry of Education published the *Religious Year Book for 1966*; and if we were to rely solely on the statistics presented in this book, we would have every reason to believe that the Japanese people are the most religious in the world. The principal data presented by the Ministry of Education can be examined on Table 1 overleaf.

It should be noted that these statistics on the total number of believers (139,607,789) include only those religions or sects which are officially recognized by the Ministry of Education. If we include other religious groups, the number rises to 155,905,502, which is seemingly impossible since we know that the Japanese population in 1966 numbered only about 100,000,000.

There is, however an easy explanation for this

apparent contradiction. The first and most basic reason is that a Japanese usually belongs to both Shintoism and Buddhism. Secondly, a great majority of the people who now belong to the new religions continue to give their names as followers of the traditional sects to which their families belonged and to which they themselves belonged before they embraced their new faith. And thirdly, there are no objective criteria for counting the number of believers. In many instances the fact that a person's name is enrolled in some religion or sect does not mean that such a person believes in that religion or sect.

Table 1: Religious Sects and Their Adherents

Religion	Sects	Believers
Shintoism	143	67,020,834
Shinto-Temples	16	54,657,376
Sectarian	127	12,363,458
Buddhism	165	67,200,117
Tendai	20	4,317,065
Shingon	48	11,871,405
Jodo	27	17,541,344
Zen	23	4,660,366
Nichiren	38	27,419,129
Nara	·7	1,219,992
Other	2	170,876
Christianity	40	636,123
Catholicism	1	289,177
Orthodoxy	1	8,983
Protestantism	38	377,963
Other Religions	28	4,750,655
Total	376	139,607,789

The Ministry of Education states that its statistics are not based on answers by individuals, but on the census which each religious group presents every year, and the criteria that each of these observes in the exact determination of its number of followers vary greatly. For example, we know that the Sōka Gakkai takes a census of its followers by families, and to number everyone in a family as Sōka Gakkai believers simply because one member belongs to this religion is to employ what seems to be a very elastic standard. Another hard fact is that the new religions, for the sake of propaganda, claim a much larger number of believers than they actually have. Morioka Kiyomi, noted Japanese sociologist on religion, believes that, in the case of the new religions particularly, "the actual numbers are estimated to be less than half of what is claimed."

In view of the various reasons that account for the apparent inaccuracy of the Ministiry of Education figures, we think a more realistic number of followers of Japanese religions can be deduced only from the results obtained in numerous religious surveys. Until the present the only nationwide investigations that could be accepted as credible, because of the strict procedures involved, were the ones conducted by the Institute of Statistics in 1953, 1958, and 1963. The results of those investigations showed that the number of Japanese believers fluctuated between 30 and 35 percent of the total population.

If the problem of accurately determining the number of Japanese believers is so complex, it can well be imagined how enormously difficult is the task of attempting to analyze the content of Japanese religious beliefs, the attitudes and motivations that underlie religious practice, and the various rites and healing superstitions (one of the chief reasons for the success of the new religions) so widespread in many sectors of Japanese society. The lack of rational logic in the religious field and the part which sentiment plays in the religiousness of the Japanese are in themselves deserving of a separate study. The concepts of spirit, divinity, life hereafter, the relationship between God and man or between gods and man—all the concepts that we would call transcendental—are extremely confusing, and it seems almost impossible to present them in a synthesis of religious thought and doctrines. Are their religions monistic, polytheistic, pantheistic, or atheistic? For most Japanese this problem seems senseless. They are not concerned about the ontological problems of their religions; what is important is religion as a practice, a cult. The concrete, the intuitive, the useful, the inner experience, the conviviality of the group—these are what they consider the values of their religions.

Obviously we cannot be satisfied with simply knowing the approximate percentage of believers in Japan. We wish to have a full knowledge of the religious practices and attitudes of those believers, as well as a knowledge of the attitudes toward religion of nonbelievers and an analysis of their motivations. A full understanding of Japanese religious situations in the postwar years requires a profound and detailed survey, one that would analyze the believing as well as the unbelieving public.

In an admittedly very imperfect way, we have attempted to carry out this investigation—first with university youth, who are the hope and future of Japan; and secondly with males between the ages of twenty and forty residing in the large cities. They are the generation which attained maturity in the postwar years, and in addition to having experienced the sociological and cultural changes in Japan during these twenty-two years, they are witnesses to the great social phenomenon of the flight from the countryside to the cities, a migration which usually produces major consequences in the religious life of an urban population.

Student: "Since I am still young I believe in neither Jesus nor Buddha."

*Student: "Religion puts our hearts at rest and adds
greater dimensions to our daily lives."*

FIRST STUDY
RELIGIOUS ATTITUDES OF JAPANESE YOUTH

The surveyors were conscious of the difficulty of formulating questions relative to the usually ambiguous term "religion" without prejudging its content or rendering it irrelevant to the actual attitudes held by students. To avoid possible bias or pointless questioning, the authors first made a content analysis of papers written for a religious class by six hundred students of Sophia University. This provided a workable range of basic ideas on religion common to the group, which the authors then checked against studies and surveys which had been made by various other research institutes.

Inquiries were sent to 104 universities all over Japan, and of these, 76 reported their own research discoveries over the last ten years. Finally, after a careful reading of relevant literature in the religious field, 143 possible questions to be included in the questionnaire were drawn up. The survey technique was based on Likert's method of "summated rating." It was important that the questions included in the questionnaire have a high coefficient of validity and reliability—that is, that they really *measured* certain attitudes and *only* those attitudes. For this reason, a substantial number of experts were consulted and only those questions receiving practically unanimous endorsement by the experts were retained for use in the survey. Through a pilot test which measured "known groups," and an "item analysis" which determined the degree to which a question actually revealed validity, the list of 143 possible questions was trimmed down to 36 valid questions.

METHODS USED IN THIS SURVEY

Precautionary steps also guided the crucial work of selecting a reliable sampling of students. Out of a combined total of 250 faculties in 118 universities in an area covering Tokyo, Kanagawa, Chiba, and Saitama prefectures, 67 faculties in 46 universities were chosen (according to the "replicated sampling method"); this yielded a total sampling of 6,586 university students.

The questionnaire was mailed out on June 10, 1966, to 6,586 students; 277 questionnaires were returned because of incorrect addresses. Of the 6,309 who received them, a surprising 59.18 percent, or 3,734, responded immediately. Of the remaining 40 percent, about one third of the 2,852 nonresponding students were chosen at randon (921 students) for "promotion" by *sokutatsu* (special delivery letter), *dempoo* (telegram), and up to three visits by field workers. Those reached in this manner numbered 741 and of these, 582 responded. We consider these as validly representative of the 2,852 who failed to answer the first letter and therefore multiply 582 by three: 1,746.

In tabulating and reporting the data, however, we distinguished the immediate responses from those of the students "upon whom it was necessary to exert some moral pressure to obtain responses." To further assist readers in relating the responses to their own experiences and interest, the results are differentiated in terms of Sophia students and those of the 44 universities, between male and female students, as well as on a broad spectrum according to university, faculty, geographical background, high school completed, personal ideals, and religious affiliation.

The total of those answering of the first group was 3,734; of the second group 1,746 (582 x 3). This total (5,480) is more than 90 percent of all who had received the questionnaire. From this number we rejected 93 answers as not valid because the students did not belong to the faculties chosen for the sampling. Of these, 48 belong to the first group; 45 to the second. Deducting only 15 from the second group because it is a representative one third (making 567), we have a total of 5,387 students.

Furthermore, if we are to assume that those whom we were unable to contact would not introduce any bias on the value of the survey and, on the contrary, if we are to assume further the possibility of a bias among the potential subjects from the two universities that declined to cooperate with us (213 students), as well as among those who absolutely refused to fill in the questionnaire, then statistical calculations indicate that the number of the respondents among the 567 should be multiplied by 4.4 to arrive at the real value of the responses. From this, we would find that of the 6,799 who composed the total original sample, we know the replies of 3,686 plus 567 x 4.4, or 6,180. Of these 5,178 are men and 1,002 are women.

The percentage of young men who confess to some religious belief is indeed small—only 7.6 percent— which means that of the total 5,178 young men who answered the questionnaire, a mere 397 follow some religion as part of their way of life. This number includes even those whose religious convictions are purely personal and not in accordance with any of the formally established religious groups. Explicitly denying all religious beliefs are 4,670 young men who constitute 90.2 percent of our male sample; while 111, or 2.1 percent of the whole male sector, did not reply at all.

The percentage of young women who have some religious belief is slightly higher: 12.9 percent of the female sector of the entire sample (1,002). Those

Table 2: Religious Affiliation of Student Respondents

Religion	Men 397		Women 130	
	No.	%	No.	%
Catholicism	29	0.56	26	2.59
Protestantism	130	2.51	59	5.88
Buddhism				
No sect specified	34	0.65	13	1.29
Jōdoshinshū	21	0.40	1	0.10
Jōdoshū	13	0.25	1	0.10
Zenshū	31	0.59	1	0.10
Nichirenshū	22	0.42	1	0.10
Shingonshū	10	0.19	4	0.39
Other sects	9	0.17	0	0.00
Shintoism	17	0.32	6	0.59
New Religions				
Buddhist				
Sōka Gakkai*	39	0.75	13	1.29
Risshōkōseikai	6	0.11	0	0.00
Shintoist				
Tenrikyō	7	0.13	0	0.00
Konkōkyō	2	0.03	0	0.00
Independent				
Seichō no ie	4	0.07	2	0.19
P. L. Kyōdan	5	0.09	1	0.10
Personal Religion	18	0.34	2	0.19
Totals:				
Christians	159	3.07	85	8.48
Buddhists	140	2.70	21	2.09
Shintoists	17	0.32	6	0.59
New Religions	63	1.21	16	1.59
Personal Religion	18	0.34	2	0.19
Total:	397	7.66	30	2.96

*Nichiren Shōshū

who admit to no faith at all constitute 86.4 percent.
Those who failed to respond to the question comprise
0.7 percent.

What are these religions professed by 7.6 percent of the young men and 12.9 percent of the young women? In Table 2 we show in detail the distribution of student believers according to the religion they follow.

What is remarkable about the figures shown in the chart is the percentage of Christians. For the entire population of Japan, the percentage is about 0.7 percent—that is, about 700,000 Protestants and Catholics. However, among the university students in the sample, 3.07 percent of the males and 8.48 percent of the females call themselves Christians. Equally surprising is the relatively tiny group who follow the new Japanese religions, which include the Sōka Gakkai, with an affiliation of several million Japanese families. These data confirm other results which reveal that among the university population there is a lack of interest in the new religions and a tendency, when evaluating the various religions, to show the most regard for either Christianity or Buddhism, which they consider serious religions.

The most representative attitude of the typical *Negative attitudes* Japanese student is his inclination to believe that religion is completely unnecessary for those who have confidence in themselves, for the strong-willed, and for those who know how to meet and to solve their problems without recourse to external support. Many openly admit that they themselves do not feel sufficiently self-confident to abandon religion altogether. But deep down in their hearts lies a powerful aversion to overt dependency on any religion. It would appear that Japanese students have some sort of socio-psychological block against making what seems to them a public admission of personal weakness.

Following are some responses of young men concerning this statement:

Religion is unnecessary for those who have self-confidence.

1. The man who relies on religion is a weak man. A strong man does not need religion. I would even go so far as to say that religion makes a man weak.
2. I think that religion is unnecessary for those who are living strongly; it becomes a powerful, saving God for the weakling.
3. If a man has a strong will, it can be said that religion is a useless thing.
4. Religion is unnecessary for a man of strong will.
5. Don't those people who depend on religion do so because they lack self-confidence? At least I want myself to become a strong personality.
6. Isn't a believer somehow weak as a human being?
7. If somebody is determined to develop his own self, that is enough, even if he does not believe at all.
8. For a man who in a relentless self-scrutiny advances toward the future, there is no objection for him not to have religion.

If religion is looked upon as nothing more than an institution founded by man to fill the psychological needs of other men and to give support to the human heart, it is not strange to find that more than 70 percent of both men and women students consider religious choice a matter of personal taste. Religion is something purely subjective and relative. The question of religion does not concern the fundamental truth or falsity of its doctrines, or of the faith on which these are based; rather it is a question of how much comfort and relief it can offer man. The criteria of truth and objectivity do not enter into the selection of one religion over another; consequently the matter of joining a religion, of accepting faith, depends exclusively on the feelings of each person. Religion belongs purely to the sphere of sentiment and feeling, which should dictate whether religion is necessary or not. It is senseless to speak of the existence of God; faith is nothing but an attitude taken by a man who, impelled by his feelings, decides that for convenience, or some other reason, it is better for him to believe in a particular religion. Man should not go to the bother of trying to decide whether this or that religion is good or bad, so long as he finds in the faith he has chosen a feeling of well-being and satisfaction.

Such are the attitudes displayed by the young men of our survey. We quote some of their remarks in reaction to the statements implying those attitudes.

The decision to acknowledge religion or not depends only on a man's feelings and moods.

1. Religion is necessary, depending upon a man's feelings and moods.
2. I know that there are many people who follow God. As they see it, he is someone who watches over and encourages them. But I think it all depends upon a man's emotional makeup.
3. Japanese people accept religion in an intuitive and sensible way, and are deficient in believing in religion on a rational basis.
4. Religion is something in the realm of emotion, in the realm of relief from anxiety.
5. From beginning to end, religion is an emotional thing.

6. For the man who believes in God, it is not a matter of knowing God's existence, but rather the point is that he recognizes God in relation to himself—that is, he thinks of God as existing because God is a help to his personal happiness.

7. Religion is something that enables you, when you are in distress, to go to a Shintoist or Buddhist temple or to a church and talk about your troubles. Just by doing that, I think you are helped out and put back into good spirits.

8. When someone really believes in a religion, one should not put the question as to whether this is good or bad. If the man himself is satisfied, then his believing is a good thing.

There are many kinds of religion, and their viewpoints differ. Therefore, it is all right if people choose that religion which suits their own taste.

1. Personally I think that religion is a way of thinking. So, for me, the problem of the existence or nonexistence of God is without meaning. Since it is a matter of one's own thought, if this way of thinking strikes a responsive chord in me, I believe; if it doesn't, I don't believe.

2. The final choice of one among the various religions depends upon one's taste.

3. Religion is not the goal of life, but rather a means or a way. Therefore, it seems only natural that there should be all sorts of ways.

4. I think it is a good thing for people to have faith, but since tastes vary according to persons, the choice should always be free.

5. Religion is an individual problem. For the one to whom it is necessary, it is something which he must have. But for the one who has no interest in it, ultimately it will be of no use.

6. I think it is up to man to select any religion at all.

7. For those to whom religion is necessary, it is necessary. For those to whom it is not, it is not.

8. I think that religion is the support of man's heart. Therefore I don't think there is any need to limit God to one definition. In other words, no matter what each individual believes in as the support of his heart—be it God or whatever it is—I think the act itself of believing is religion.

We hasten to add, however, that although the students have these thoughts about religion, they do not necessarily possess a conscious negative attitude toward religion. To them, their attitude is one which any young man of today should have. They think that the cultured man of today has freed himself from the myth that religion possesses absolute values. But many of them also believe that an attitude of clear opposition, one that is extremely negative, is an equally erroneous appraisal of their position vis-à-vis religion. Therefore, as the statements about religion proposed to them become progressively, clearly, and explicitly negative, we should expect a corresponding decrease in the number of affirmative replies.

There are two other statements especially that are closely related to the first three previously examined. These take up religion as "an escape from reality" and as "a recourse to the gods in time of trouble." But there is an important difference; in these two expressions, the words used—*toohi, kamidanomi* (escape, recourse to the gods)— indicate to the Japanese that we are dealing with a negative attitude relative to religion. On the other hand, in the previous statements the core words employed—*jishin, kimochi to kanjoo, hadani au* (self-confidence, feelings and moods, what suits my own taste)—are words which, to the Japanese way of thinking, do not in themselves have any negative connotation. Only among some 40 to 50 percent of the students is there a clear feeling that religion is disreputable, especially when they consider it as just an escape from reality that bespeaks open cowardice in the face of the world and life's problems. Religion is nothing but man's psychological gimmick to which he has recourse in time of tribulation—*kurushii toki no kamidanomi*.

Following are some responses to the statements proposed:

Religion is a means of escaping from the troubles of the real world.

1. I think that the so-called believer is a man running away from real life—very much as a coward would.

2. Religion amounts to nothing more than man's escape from present reality and the problem of conscience.

3. Religion is both a cringing dependence upon something or someone else and a flight from the real world.

4. Nowadays, in the midst of mechanized society, religion is nothing more than one way of getting away from everyday reality.

5. Religion is but a means of escape. The attitude of "looking to God for salvation" means to stop looking at reality and to give up all personal efforts. And I think that the saying "what is beyond the power of men can be achieved with God's help" is also a form of escapism.

6. Even though I may have to face hard times, I'm certainly not going to go running the escape route of faith.

7. Religion estranges man from the problems of society, removes him from the present world, and satisfies his longing for an undisturbed life, making for him an ideal, individualistic, little paradise of his own.

8. Shouldn't we define religion as running away from the real world?

Religion is nothing more than calling upon the gods in time of trouble.

1. As proverbs such as "The drowning man snatches at a straw" and "Call on the gods when trouble comes" illustrate, religion is a thing men resort to in order to struggle through hardships.

2. "Call on the gods when troubles comes"—that is me exactly! I cannot bring myself to believe in God with heart and soul.

3. "Call on the gods when trouble comes" sums up completely my view of religion.

4. The common characteristic of the various religions consists in the tendency men have, when faced with misfortunes and troubles, of wanting to depend upon something. Following this tendency, man gets religion; and relying on religion, he can face the misfortune.

5. When our heart is confronted with suffering because of its yearning for the existence of something greater than itself to depend on, it gives birth to God.

6. Those who have incurable diseases, those who are poor, those who are in distress, that is, all those who are troubled in heart, seem to cling fast to "Call on the gods in time of trouble."

7. As the proverb "In time of trouble appeal to the gods" indicates, when one is pushed to the wall, one gets an inkling of the existence of God.

8. When one's own strength utterly fails—for example, in times of sickness or in danger of death—one yearns for God's existence and begs his help.

About 35 percent of the subjects affirm that religion is opposed to, and contradicts, science and reason; consequently, it is for those men of low culture who are ignorant of the fundamentals of science.

Religion is in contradiction to science and reason.

1. There can be no coexistence between science and religion. Going against science, which is in quest of the true image of man and of nature, religion is something artificial made by man himself.

2. As for the unscientific matter of God's existence or nonexistence, I have no interest at all. To argue about God's existence in an era as scientifically advanced as the present is meaningless.

3. Someone like me who is studying rational social science cannot bear to believe in something as irrational as religion.

4. Since today religion is looked upon as something unscientific and not in conformity with the age, the average man cannot accept it.

5. Here in Japan we learn from grade school on that science and religion are incompatible.

6. In a scientifically advanced era like the present, is there really in existence a being like God, so immensely surpassing man? Rather than doubting about it, one could hardly say otherwise than that thinking in such a way would be foolish. I think that any man who believes in God is a fool. No, rather than that, I would say that I pity such a person.

7. That religion thwarts the progress of science is a historical fact. *Negative attitudes*

8. I think that religion and science are opposed. Science bit by bit explains the systematic principles which govern nature, its mysteries, and its order. The origin of all this (especially the origin of life) no one at all understands yet. So as for myself in the face of all this, I can only bow my head and say, "I don't know."

It is important to know that the rest—that is, the remaining 65 percent—with their "don't know" replies to this question, or even with their negative answers, do not necessarily believe that what religion preaches is in accord with what science teaches. Rather, a deep analysis of their attitudes shows us that such replies mean that the respondents accept the theory of the two truths, separatings religious truth from scientific truth. What is truth in religion could be denied in science, and vice versa. Religion and science are two separate worlds, each with its viewpoint and criteria, and it is absurd to want to compare them. As an illustration, here is what a young Japanese says about miracles:

It is only natural to deny all miracles from the scientific viewpoint. Therefore the discussions between scientists and theologians about miracles are unnecessary and meaningless. But a person who has faith, and as a result of his faith believes in miracles, will be not at all influenced by the fact that miracles are proved to be scientifically impossible. The person who believes in God can possess his world of faith completely different from his world of science.

The students who believe that religion is an impediment to personality development constitute about 25 percent of the sample. This group thinks that religion at least lessens the vigorous spirit of independence and freedom, and is a barrier to the growth of one's originality and other faculties. Religion, they believe, gives rise to a common type of human being who lacks true individuality; it does not tend to favor and promote leadership qualities. For such students it is difficult to conceive of themselves in the full bloom of life acquiring a belief in religion. We offer typical responses in reaction to two statements representing this belief:

Religion weakens one's individuality and blocks the development of one's personality.

1. Religion is a cowardly fleeing from one's self. I think that in a way it is the greatest enemy of the development of personality. Why? Well, instead of facing distress and worry headon, wrestling with it fair and square, you try to evade it with prayers and adoration, making no effort to really use your intelligence.

2. We should have firm convictions; but I can't help thinking that religion turns you into a weakling, dependent upon something outside yourself.

3. The truly beautiful image of man must be shaped by man himself, not by any dependence upon some other, such as God, it seems to me; for in the latter case man's personal identity is lost.

4. I never want to profess any faith becuase, as I see it, insofar as you come to believe in religion, you entangle yourself in a prearranged system of thought, and this amounts to the same thing as giving up your individuality.

5. The one who becomes a believer somehow appears maimed as a man.

6. I don't recognize the necessity of religion. I place the highest value upon personal autonomy.

7. I feel that insofar as one comes to believe in God, one becomes weak.

8. As far as thinking about religion goes, it seems to be something removed from ordinary life. Then, too, if you study religion deeply and become a believer, not only your daily life, but your thought processes also, become extremely constricted; and furthermore, in the eyes of those around you, you become some sort of special being.

It may be that religion is something fitting for old people, but for young people it is something you may take or leave.

1. Religion has no relation at all to the young people of. today. Rather than spew words about religion and the like that are of no use to the belly, it seems it would be better to use your spare time some other way.

2. Religion enervates man and strengthens his feeling of dependency. And I think that this does the greatest harm to the young. Since I am still young, I believe in neither Jesus or Buddha.

3. I consider religion to be something for old people who experience uneasiness about the world that they are on the threshold of, or for the incurably ill who are looking for some help. Therefore, as far as we healthy young people are concerned, religion is considered irrelevant.

4. In Japan has not religion come to be thought of in the minds of young people as a cane for old people?

5. When I am older than I am now, and tossed about in the storms of human life, I think I will feel deeply the need for religion as a way of calming my soul. It seems that one wants to believe in God as he advances in age. But I am still young.

6. My father had no faith or anything of that sort before, but recently I have seen him with both hands clasped, worshipping in front of the household altar. "It is because our father is also finally approaching nearer to the next world, isn't it?" my brother and I have sometimes joked.

7. When I hear of religion, I have a feeling of something outdated, something which is approached by old people. It is foolish for us young people to approach it.

The statistical data disclose a minority group comprising between 15 to 25 percent of our sample, whose attitude toward religion is one of total disdain, frank hostility, and negativeness. These students think of religion as a relic of the past, a heritage from our primitive ancestors, the fruit of man's crass ignorance. They look upon religion as pure hallucination, plain superstition, and an absurdity in the light of modern civilization. Further, they realize that history has taught that religion was, and still is, the opium of the masses, and serves as a tool of control in the hands of the powerful.

A large portion of Japanese youth recognize a series of positive values in religion. Up to this point we have examined the young men's responses to statements that were either clearly negative or, at least contained negative nuances with respect to religion. It is precisely to avoid a bias in our survey that we have endeavored to present other more affirmative statements or theses.

We do not believe we have encountered any contradictions among the replies given to the two groups of survey statements. On the contrary, we believe that they harmonize and enable us to better understand the overall religious mentality of the university freshmen. If, to the statements that contained an opinion on religion that was extremely negative, the young Japanese, with the exception of about 25 percent, responded with a more or less definite *no*, he also responded with a *no* to those statements which more positively presented religion as "something strictly necessary, as the only true way which a man should follow, as the light that directs man to the genuine truth and shows him what is truly good and beautiful." The positive replies to these statements were very few, frequently no more than 11 percent.

However, there is another series of statements that presents religion as a means of securing calm and interior peace; as one solution to the fundamental problems of human loneliness and the feeling of alienation which modern man bears deep in his soul; as a moral ideal which gives direction to his behavior. In brief, the series portrays religion as a prop for the human heart. It is a religion which makes men the center, not God.

To these postulates, the positive responses are frequently in the majority and are not opposed to the religious attitudes of the students that we discovered in the preceding pages: (1) that religion fulfills the purpose of furnishing a support for the human heart in those persons who need it and who will always be in the majority, and (2) that the individual who finds within himself such a support for living will never have any need for religion. These represent two frames of mind which are not contradictory. Actually, they complement each other.

Between 55 and 65 percent of the male sector of our sample see spiritual values in religion which man should accept and appreciate. Religion often brings inner peace to the individual who has it; it is a faithful companion in moments of solitude and gives comfort and assurance in times of tribulation and suffering. Religion offers great spiritual support during life's most miserable moments.

Religion is a good teacher in all matters concerning human moral conduct. Every religion that is a true religion must struggle for peace among all nations and for social order and welfare, while encouraging men to control their purely selfish instincts. Four statements elicited these judgments.

Religion instills peace in the depths of a man's heart.

1. By believing in religion man's heart can obtain peace.
2. By believing in religion you have a feeling of relief and become composed. And this, I think, is both profitable and necessary.
3. Religion puts our hearts at rest and adds greater dimension to our daily lives.
4. Peace of heart is something extremely important for man's happiness, and I think this is what religion aims at.
5. In order to achieve peace of heart, religion is necessary.
6. While one is aware of the severity of the man who believes, it seems nevertheless that faith gives him peace and tranquillity.
7. Considering human life in all its aspects, you see that when a man believes, his unrest over his defects is remedied and he gets peace of heart.

8. Fundamentally, religion is that which gives us peace of heart. Positive attitudes

Religion saves man from his emptiness and loneliness.
1. Isn't it true that we know of God's existence when we recognize that man is loneliness?
2. When man feels his own lack of strength or his strong isolation, he searches for God or Buddha. Therefore I don't deny religion.
3. Religion is nothing more than a means for man to escape from his own personal loneliness.
4. I consider religion to be something which solves the question of man's isolation.
5. I think the source of religion is man's search for some absolute being on which he can rely to save himself from his fear of death and feeling of loneliness. At this moment man invents God. Therefore I think of religion as one aspect of man's weakness.
6. I wonder whether religion in the final analysis does not exist but as a refuge for the lonely heart of man.
7. Man is sometimes overcome with terrible feelings of loneliness. At such times he clings to something having absolute power and under its protection he wants to secure his safety. In this way religion and faith are born.

Religion is extremely worthwhile as a support of man's heart.
1. Man, facing his existence, finds support in religion and makes it a place of repose.
2. I think it is a good thing that by relying on God people obtain support and peace of heart.
3. I don't deny religion in all of its aspects, as I acknowledge its value as a spiritual support.

27

4. I think that religion is important both to steady the heart when it is wavering and also to build man's character.

5. I don't want to deny religion, because it is more convenient for man to create a God he can rely on than to rely on man.

6. If there is someone who can be happy by believing in and relying on God, I think it is a very good thing.

7. All men are weak in some way and are looking for some kind of support. If thereby a man comes to believe in a certain sense, it is perfectly all right.

8. The man who is looking for something to rely on becomes predisposed to believe in God. Isn't it a very good thing if by this belief his heart is relieved and a smile appears on his face?

Religion gives discipline and moral training to the whole man. It can make a great contribution to the realization of peace among mankind.

1. I don't have any faith but I am of the opinion that man should have some interest in religion because, from the moral point of view, it has many good points.

2. Because many of religion's concepts are morally good for us, in order to progress in life we must clearly understand this religion and then act according to it. Those with faith can live a better life than those without faith.

3. For me religion is nothing more than a means to good moral behavior.

4. Could it be possible to have moral education without a religious foundation?

5. If one were to specify the purpose of religion, I think it is peace and happiness for mankind.

6. At the present time one cannot talk about reli- *Positive attitudes*
gion and ignore the social community. That is
to say, I believe that religion and society are
mutually related, and should contribute to the
happiness of mankind.
7. In a world like the present one, I think that
religion must greatly contribute to world peace.
8. Since contemporary civilization has become
rather advanced, I think that if we follow religion (true religion), we can hold in check contemporary dangers too.

The very same group—55 to 65 percent of our
sample—as a logical consequence of their prior attitudes would tell us that man and society in general
would stand to lose tremendously if some day religion were to disappear from the face of the earth.

As previously mentioned, the fact that this group
recognizes the positive values of religion does not
mean that they accept them on an objective and absolute plane; instead, most accept them only on
subjective, psychological, and moral levels. This interpretation of their positive responses is confirmed
by their statements expressing approval of the opinions set forth in the survey.

Thirty percent of the students reveal an attitude of
great respect for religion, and we believe that there is
in them at least a subconscious wish to someday become a believer. They feel that religion, far from
being a barrier to the full development of one's personality, is a most effective means to, and an almost
necessary tool for, man's improvement and conquest
of self. It is very probable that these young men will
continue through life without any religion. If they
do, it will be because of their environment and the
lack of opportunities to study more deeply the prob-

lem of religion—although plain laziness and insufficient moral courage to start along new ways could also be responsible for their failure to make a religious commitment. Even within this group there is detectable a subconscious fear of the mere idea of turning believer. They desire it, but they know that such a step would require a radical change in their personal attitudes. Up to the present, the development of "self" has been practically the only goal greatly valued by the Japanese young man, and the one for which he has struggled so tenaciously. He realizes that upon turning believer, religion—or more concretely, God—has to take primacy in his life over and above his egoism and ahead of his tremendous egocentrism. The mere thought of having to accept submission to God often becomes the reason why the young man's subconscious desire to become a believer is frustrated and never manifests itself. We offer some of the comments.

It can be said that a life based on religion deserves respect.

1. I consider people who have faith, who pray to God, who avoid evil desires, who lead a modest life, to be great men.
2. I myself do not know what I will believe in the future. Perhaps I will have no faith. Still I feel that a man who believes in a religion is some sort of a strong person.
3. I see a good number of believers dedicatedly carrying on a life of service and I consider them to be excellent people.
4. I feel envious of a man who can really believe from his heart in a religion, and I myself would like to come to such a state.

5. I become envious when I see the cheerful life of Positive attitudes believers.

6. When I see people who believe in religion, I become envious. Why is this? Because they separate themselves from this fickle world and thereby come to possess something they can trust.

7. Because the necessity for more levelheadedness in today's complex society, I think it would be good if man attached more importance to religion.

8. I have a feeling of envy and a lot of respect for a fervent believer and a certain sadness at my own lack thereof.

Some 18 to 19 percent go even beyond this in their approval of religion. They look upon religion as the great teacher who enables man to share in the great fundamental truths about mankind and who leads him to realize the values of beauty and goodness in their most sublime forms.

Religion, which makes a man grasp the highest truth, beauty, and goodness, is most important for man.

1. I search for God not so much as a "support for my heart" but rather because I love truth.

2. Isn't the heart, which is searching for truth and kneels down before it, touching the essence of religion?

3. Religion must be a signpost which points the way to truth.

4. Religion necessarily comes into existence when man looks at the beauty of nature and considers all the mysterious phenomena of the universe.

5. Man is in pursuit of an infinite beauty. This pursuit is religion.

Up to what point do the young men of this group hold an objective view of religion? What is the extent of the value they place on religion? These are questions we find quite difficult to answer. Some findings seem to indicate that there are many who, though admitting and accepting in their minds these values of religion, are emotionally unaffected by it except superficially. And which facts lead us to this conclusion? First of all, the number of believers does not go beyond 8 percent, and this includes all those who profess some faith or another, as well as those whose faith is of a strictly personal nature unassociated with any single religious institution. This figure of 8 percent is unrealistic, for it includes those students who answered that they belong to some sect of Shintoism or Buddhism but who later admitted that by such replies they meant only that it was their family's religion, which did not necessarily mean that they themselves professed such a faith. In the second place, if this admitted interest in religion were really deeply felt, the young men would employ some means or other to investiage the religious question; yet the majority will not take the trouble to do so. It is doubtless that if they were offered an opportunity for religious investigation they would grasp it; but they would not seek such an opportunity on their own. In addition, the answers to one of the questions, which we shall analyze presently, led us to the same interpretation.

Only 11 percent believe that religion is necessary for every man. We do not speak here of necessity in the psychological sense but of necessity in a deeper sense—that is, that every man should follow the path of religion because it is the best and only way for him to attain the fullness of his manhood. Only 11 percent accepted this opinion.

Finally, we have only the last attitude of the students to discuss. This reveals that in a great majority of cases there is a deep-down interest and some respect for religion, even though their words deny this. Fully 73 percent replied that at least once in his lifetime every man should study the question of religion. Such a response would hardly have been forthcoming if there were absolutely no interest in religion, or if religion were considered trivial or of no importance at all. Therefore, if we set aside the 25 percent who form the minority group that has shown a genuinely negative attitude toward religion, we find that the rest consist of those who are not sure of their religious ideas but who at least tacitly admit their ignorance and who have a definite suspicion that religion may actually have more importance than they now attribute to it. Furthermore, these students believe that they must look more seriously and deeply into the question of religion if only for cultural and historical reasons.

Positive attitudes

The analysis presented in the preceding pages refers to the general student population. But this student group cannot be considered entirely homogeneous. Although all those included in the survey are Japanese, their cultural, familial, and educational backgrounds—and, indeed, their individual personalities—could be so distinctly different as to exert a marked influence on their religious attitudes. To understand and measure the influence of such differences, we initiated a second analysis.

Qualified results of the survey

In this second study we divided the students into categories based on the following ten criteria which we believed could have some significance in the analysis of their religious attitudes:

1. Geographic region of origin.
2. School attended for secondary education.

3. Social position and occupation of the head of the family.
4. Parents' religious attitudes.
5. Whether they entered the university immediately after finishing high school, or waited one or two years before enrolling in college.
6. The university they now attend.
7. The department or faculty to which they belong.
8. Goal in life.
9. Experience of religious prayer.
10. Profession of faith.

Not all the criteria proved to be of equal value in determining the religious attitudes of the students. According to some, the results as gleaned from the responses were quite homogeneous; according to others, there were notable and significant differences.

School attended for secondary education: The young men in the male sector of our sample who received their secondary education in public institutions number 3,273; the total of those who finished this education in private, nonsectarian colleges is 1,481. The results obtained in the two groups are so similar that it is difficult to detect the slightest difference between them that might serve to contrast their respective religious attitudes.

There is another group of 424 young men who had come from religious institutions—that is, Christian, Buddhist, and Shintoist colleges, and schools founded by the new religious sects. The men who received their high-school training at these institutions do not generally follow the religion of their schools. Furthermore, religious training is not obligatory even in such institutions. The education given by these schools, however, would ordinarily be oriented according to the pedagogical principles of the respective religions. Thus, it is to be expected that the men trained at these educational centers would have been subjected to some special influence which, in turn, could influence their religious outlook.

Let us now compare the results gathered from studies of the men trained in Catholic, Buddhist, and Protestant schools. (Those educated in the schools of other religious groups total a mere 42, which is too small a number to establish valid percentage comparison bases.) We shall then compare these results with the total results from our entire sample.

It is obvious that the differences between these three groups and the rest of the majority group of 4,754 young men are statistically significant. The differences, which often vary from 15 to 20 percent—and at times even reach 30 percent—underscore the degree of positiveness in attitudes toward religion of the young men trained in religious institutions. It then becomes undeniable that in those educational centers these youths were indeed influenced positively relative to religion.

There are also differences within the three groups themselves. In general, the percentage most favorable toward religion centered on the young men from the Christian schools.

Inside these three groups, there are responses with such conspicuous variations that we should like to point them out. For example, the fourth question concerns the criterion in the choice of a religion, and states in effect that one should choose that religion which best suits his "tastes"—a criterion implicitly based on purely subjective and relativistic reasons. The affirmative replies to this statement given by the students of Catholic schools were only 58.1 percent, while similar answers from students of the Protestant and Buddhist schools reached 75.7 and 76.1 percent, respectively. In like manner, the statement that religion is something purely sentimental in nature received approval from just 20.8 percent of the group from Catholic schools, while the affirmative replies of the other two groups registered 38.3 percent and 41.9 percent, respectively.

In a similar manner, the percentage of the young men from Catholic schools who feel that people whose lives and attitudes are based upon religion deserve every respect is 65 percent, considerably greater than the 51.4 percent of the Protestant group and the 45.3 percent of the Buddhist group.

Replies eliciting a differential of approximately 10 percent definitely indicate a distinct attitude variation with regard to religion and are not due to mere statistical chance. Even smaller differences, when they constantly appear in the answers to almost all of the questions, can also be indicative of really different attitudes.

We observed the same phenomenon among the girls in our survey sample. There is, for all practical purposes, no difference between the group of 290 young women trained in private, nonsectarian institutions and the group of 545 educated in public schools. But those coming from Catholic schools (73) and Protestant schools (69) reveal an attitude toward religion that is definitely more positive than that of the other two groups. This difference is even more pronounced among the young women that it is among the young men. Outstanding as a group are the young women trained in schools staffed by Catholic nuns. The percentage who state that religion gives sense and direction to living and makes clear the purpose of man, is the source of encouragement for the human heart, encourages a high standard of morals, and adds

a spiritual dimension to life, is always around 80 percent. On the other hand, the group of Sister-trained
young women who think that religion is only for the
weak and the dissatisfied comprises a mere 20 percent. We have to make clear, however, that since the
number polled is a small one—only 73—we cannot
know for certain to what extent these percentages are
truly representative of the total female population
educated in such colleges. We did not include in our
study the young women trained in Buddhist and
Shintoist schools because they were a scant 23 in all.

Parents' religious attitudes: Parents' religious attitudes usually exert a strong influence on the religious attitudes of their children. In postwar Japan,
however, this influence seems to have dwindled to a
minimum in a large number of families. The end of
the last war saw practically the total disappearance of
religious instruction. As we noted earlier, not only
did religious education and instruction cease in all
schools, but even in families of believers there remain
very few parents who talk to their children about
religion and teach them the faith which they themselves practice.

The feeling that religion is a personal problem
which every individual must solve for himself has
grown enormously; consequently no one feels he has
the right to interfere in another's religious quandary.
It is now considered antidemocratic to induce children to follow any particular religion or to instruct
them in any faith; when the child grows up, he can
make up his own mind about what he wants to do, or
not do, about a personal religion. Further, it would
seem that the parents themselves have lost the self-
confidence necessary to orient their offspring in
matters touching on religion. They seem even to have
lost some of their trust in the faith that they them-

selves profess, and this naturally robs them of the capacity to lead their children in religious ways.

Of the 5,178 men in our sample, 2,841 answered that their parents were believers. Of these, only 91 are of Christian parentage divided between Catholics and Protestants. The remaining 2,750 students replied that their parents were believers in Japanese religions, but when later asked if they had received some instruction or practical education in religion, within the family circle, only 15.8 percent (436) replied in the affirmative.

After analyzing the results we came to the conclusion that in present-day Japan the mere fact of a family's belonging to some faith does not exert any significant influence on the religion of the children. Only when these children have received from the family some religious training, no matter how slight, do they frequently come to have a more positive attitude toward religion. In the girls' group we note the same results as in the group of men.

Goal in life: With increasing frequency, in the numerous surveys presently being conducted among the youth in Japan, there is usually one or more questions directed to students relating to their life's ideals. These studies guided us in formulating five life ideals or goals; from these, the subjects were asked to select the one they most preferred. If none of the five satisfied them, they were simply to indicate this fact.

The five ways of life proposed to the students are as follows:

1. To live according to my likes and interests.
2. To seek after good social position, wealth, and fame.
3. To exert myself for the good of men and society.
4. Without any special aims, to try and live satis-

fied and in harmony with the environment and the circumstances which surround me.

5. To live a clean and honest life.

Thirty-two percent of the young men chose the first proposition as their goal in life; 22 percent preferred the last; 16 percent would exert themselves for the good of society; 10 percent would try to satisfy their ambitions for wealth, fame, and prestige; 3 percent would be content to lead their lives as circumstances permitted them; and the remaining 17 percent admit to having ideals which do not agree with any of the five proposed.

Among the young women, a large number—34.5 percent—chose as their life aspirations the moral ideal of a pure and honest life. The second largest group, 28.6 percent, would try to live according to their desires and interests; and 14.5 percent incline toward working for the good of society. A small sector, 3.3 percent would take a passive attitude toward life, and only 1.2 percent would struggle for riches and social prestige. Those whose ideals of living are not among any of the five mentioned comprise the remaining 17.9 percent.

It is clear that the responses given by the students are not mutually exclusive; their acceptance of one ideal does not necessarily mean that they reject the others. Their replies, therefore, merely indicate what to them would be the most important element in living, what human value they would give priority to, what life ideal attracts them most, and, consequently, what will guide and direct their future attitudes and conduct.

We tried to determine what relationship, if any, existed between their ideals of living on the one hand, and their religious attitudes on the other. It is interesting to note that, among both the men and women whose preferred ideal was to work for the good of society, we find an attitude toward religion that is more favorable than that held by those who chose the first, second, and fourth ways of life. Those who placed greater emphasis on the moral aspects of life, seeking honest conduct as their primary goal, are close in their viewpoint to the altruistic group.

To simplify our remarks concerning the above findings, we shall designate these five groups as follows: Altruist Group (third way of living), Moral Group (fifth way of living), Egoist Group (first way of living), Ambitious Group (second way of living), and Passive Group (fourth way of living).

The first difference we notice is that 65 percent of the students in the Altruist Group state that they have a positive interest in religion. The percentage with some religious interest among the Egoist Group is only 44 percent and, among the Passive Group, a mere 32.4 percent. In between are the Ambitious Group, with a 48.1 percent; and the Moral Group, with a 51.3 percent. The difference between the Altruist Group and all the others, varying from 14 to 32 percent, is certainly very significant.

In the answers to the thirty-six basic questions of the survey, we frequently find in the Altruist Group a difference of 10 percent more in favor of religion compared with the Egoist, Ambitious, and Passive groups. The Moral Group shows a mental pattern very similar to that of the Altruist Group in their responses.

Experience of religious prayer: Of the males included in our survey sample, 7 percent declared that they pray and worship with great frequency. This is practically identical with the 7.6 percent sector which professes some religious faith. It is natural that their religious point of view should be vastly different from that of the group of nonbelievers, as we shall see below.

But another more numerous group of 2,211 young men, though they denied having any faith, still admitted in their answers that during moments of great difficulty in their past lives they sometimes prayed; thus they have had the religious experience of petitional praying. This group comprises 43 percent of the male sector of our survey sample.

It may seem absurd that young men without any religious faith can have such an experience. But though it is somewhat difficult to explain on purely logical grounds, it is easier to clarify on a human, psychological basis. These youths tell us there is an instinct in man which urges him to pray in times of crisis, and human experience confirms this. The young men, however, offer this explanation without stopping to think that there could be some contradiction in the idea that one can resort to prayer, and at the same time, deny the existence of a being superior to man who could listen to that prayer. Furthermore, if any were to discern such a contradiction, it would not disquiet them. What is important to them is that, when faced with difficulties in life, the experience of prayerful thoughts gives comfort and peace to the soul.

We would like to quote here a few of the many remarks we gathered while reading the young men's essays on religion. All the phrases chosen were taken from the compositions of those who have denied all religious faith.

1. At one time I had an appendix operation. On account of the great pain, I prayed in my heart, "God, please make it not be painful any more," and during the operation I also prayed that the operation would be successful.

2. Once when I caught a cold and ran a fever of almost forty centigrades, I thought I would die, and at that time I prayed to God.

3. When I was in trouble—for instance, at the time of the entrance examinations or when I became sick—it is a fact that at those times I felt like relying on God.

4. In instances when I cannot do anything by my own power, or when something suddenly happens, I often think of God. For me to do this is a real contradiction.

5. When I don't have any problems at all, I don't have the least thought about religion. But when an emergency arises, of course I think of God.

6. I have never met God. And yet, even though I can't explain how, I place a lot of confidence in the proverb, "In adverse times, pray to God."

7. When in trouble, everybody will ask for God's help.

8. Even a man without any faith will, when in trouble, feel like crying, "Oh, God!"

All the above-quoted excerpts show us that the young men, during trying periods in their lives (which at their age almost invariably means examinations in school or illness) have tried to lighten their worries and lessen their sufferings by means of prayer. As they themselves say, it is purely subjective prayer, without foundation in any religious faith; but, after all, those are moments of religious experience.

An extraordinarily interesting fact we have discovered is that this group of 2,211 young men, who have admitted this prayer experience even without any religious faith, has shown a religious attitude that is more favorable than that of the group who said that they almost never prayed (2,203 students—39 percent of the male population); and, a fortiori, their attitude was much more favorable than that of those male students who do not remember ever having prayed in their lives (589 students—11 percent). The answers given by these three groups to the 36 questions in the survey are in almost perfect correlation with their experience of prayer; namely, their religious attitudes are more positive in direct proportion to their previous experience of prayer.

The brief religious experiences, consisting of a few, haphazard prayer-thoughts, have left their mark upon the souls of these young men, by imprinting a memory of inner peace of mind. This explains why their attitudes toward religion are frequently 15 to 20 percent more positive than those of their fellow students who had never had such an experience. This is an interesting phenomenon in religious psychology.

We have found this same extraordinary fact among the university women. Nineteen percent worship and pray frequently; this exceeds the percentage found in the group of actual believers. Those who have had occasional prayer experiences number 495, which represents 49.5 percent of the total female sector of our sample; the ones who have rarely prayed are 265, or 26.5 percent of the entire female group; while only 50 admit never having prayed at all. The difference between these three groups is equally remarkable for maintaining the parallel proportions observed among the boys' groups.

Profession of faith: We now come to the most critical criterion in the determination and differentiation of the religious attitudes of our subjects. It is obvious that those who profess some religious faith will have a more favorable attitude toward religion than those who do not believe in any religion.

What are the religious attitudes of the different

groups of believers? To statements of an extremely negative nature—such as "Religion, in our present state of advanced civilization, is close to superstition," "Religion is nothing but a drug which makes man submissive and resigned," "Religion is founded on man's hallucinations," "Religion is born of man's ignorance," etc.—the percentage of those who agree fluctuates among the Catholics from 0 to 2.5 percent; among the Protestants, from 0 to 6 percent; and among the Buddhists, from 4 to 11 percent.

Other statements of a negative character, although not as negative as the ones appearing in the preceding paragraph, postulate that religion offers man a psychological escape from the miseries and trials of life. They further indicate that religion is opposed to science and acts as a barrier to the development of a strong personality. The percentage of affirmative replies to these statements rises a bit in the various groups: for the Catholics, it goes from 5 to 10 percent; for the Protestants, from 8 to 16 percent; and for the others from 5 to 10 percent. Finally remaining to be analyzed are the responses elicited by the following statements: "Religion is unnecessary for those who have self-confidence"; "For a person who is satisfied with his life, religion is not really necessary"; "The decision to acknowledge religion or not depends merely on a man's feelings and moods"; "There are many kinds of religions, and their viewpoints differ. Therefore it is all right if people choose that religion which suits their own taste."

As explained in the general analysis, the young Japanese do not read into the approval of these statements any clearly negative attitude. To them, the postulates are indicative only of the purely subjective aspects. Religion is for the weak and those dissatisfied with life; and it is not based upon reason, but merely

on human emotions. The selection of one religion or
another is simply a matter of personal taste. These
opinions, widespread in Japanese society, have had a
strong impact on believers. Of the university young
men who are Christians, between 10 and 20 percent
also think of religion as something that is purely subjective and relative. These youths may be those with
insufficient Christian upbringing, or those who were
baptized as small children but received no subsequent
religious instruction; they may be those who were
directly influenced by what they read or by what
they had talked about with their friends. Whatever
the explanation, the fact remains that this group
believes and affirms, in the same manner as the nonbelievers, that religion is unncessary for those who
have sufficient self-confidence to feel that they themselves are capable of handling any difficulties that
may arise in life. The percentage of Catholics who
share this feeling is lower than the percentage in the
other two groups.

*Qualified results
of the survey*

We notice higher percentages for the non-Christian
religious groups—that is, the Buddhist, Shintoist, and
new-religion groups (between 34 and 66 percent of
those believers respond affirmatively to those statements that derogate religion). We are not too sur-
prised by such data; the phenomenon can be under-
stood in the light of the relativism and syncretism
that have always been predominant characteristics of
all Japanese religions.

To the majority of the statements favorable to religion, the percentage of positive answers among the
Christian group goes beyond 80 percent, and even 90
percent, at times. Among the non-Christian groups it
lies between 60 and 80 percent. But there are two
statements which are considered to be the most positive relative to religion. The first is that religion is

what leads a man to the knowledge of the most fundamental and sublime truths as well as to the recognition of supreme goodness and beauty. The second is that every man should follow the way of religion. Between 20 and 30 percent of the Catholics, and between 30 and 50 percent of the Protestants, do not agree that religion is necessary to man; neither do they consider religion very important as the source of genuine and fundamental truths. Among the other religious groups between 50 and 60 percent deny those statements.

Student: "Go to a Shintoist or Buddhist temple or to a church when you are in distress? I think you are helped and put back into good spirits."

Student: "The truly beautiful image of man must be shaped by man himself, not by dependence upon some other, such as God."

COMPLEMENTARY PILOT SURVEYS

There are other themes of prime importance that fall within the scope of a survey on the religious attitudes of university students. We therefore conducted several studies of a limited nature among some student groups at Sophia University to learn what concepts they hold of God and of life in the hereafter.

These minor surveys do not have the representative value of the general survey which we have been analyzing up to this point; we were merely engaged in some pilot studies. However, the results we obtained seem interesting and we believe that they can lead us into a better understanding of the problems we were investigating. On the other hand, we want to point out that the results we obtained in the pilot studies of religion among the Sophia University students did not differ appreciably from those obtained in the general survey. We can therefore assume that the results obtained in these limited investigations would not differ much from the results which would be gathered in another general and definitive survey on the same problems.

We conducted this study with 111 first-year students in the Faculty of Law and the Faculty of Sciences (49 from Law, 62 from Sciences) of Sophia University in early May 1965, two weeks after the beginning of the school year. It was carried out during the students' weekly period in religion.

Existence of God and ideas about God

The first statements were of a fundamental character calculated to discover what their thinking was with respect to belief in the existence of God. They were:

(1) God did not create man; man created God.
(2) God does not exist merely as an idea in man's thought; he has a real existence.

To the first statement, 82 young men gave their approval, which is 73.8 percent of the respondents; 13 of the group—11.6 percent—replied in the negative; while 16, or 14.5 percent, answered that they "don't know." Reactions to the second statement show insignificant variations. Only 10 students (9 percent) answered affirmatively; 80 (72 percent) denied the statement; and 21 (18.9 percent) said that they "don't know."

Their answers confirm, in the first place, the statistical data gathered in the general survey as to the number of believers and nonbelievers. It should be noted, despite the slight difference, that in the case of answers to the negative statement—that is, the statement that man created God—the percentage of those who deny it is 2.6 percent more than the percentage of those who state positively that they believe in the existence of God.

Those who clearly deny the existence of God comprise between 72 and 74 percent of the students. Of those who doubt God's existence—approximately 19 percent—we think there are many who, despite their inability to affirm that God exists, see reasons for, and the possibility of, the existence of God. This group, together with the group of believers—about 9 percent—correlates with the group of students in the general survey who show a decidedly positive and favorable attitude toward religion.

Because of the vagueness in Japanese thinking about God, we attempted to propound to the young university men a series of simple definitions that might enable them to select the image, or images, which were closest to the mental picture created in their minds upon hearing the word "God." The first two questions asked them directly about their beliefs in the existence or nonexistence of God. In order to understand just what God they were accepting or rejecting in their replies, we added those other ques- tions which analyzed the idea of God. We instructed the young men that in replying to these last queries they were to forget completely whether or not they believed in the existence of God, since we were only attempting to discover the most dominant idea they had of God.

Let us now see what these students have for an image of God, as disclosed by their affirmative replies to the various ideas or concepts of God in the survey definitions which most nearly approximated what was in their minds.

About 45 percent seem to conceive of God as being very similar to the God of Christianity—that is, a God who is one, absolute, and personal. But most of these young men would not agree that this mental picture represents a being who really exists but only that it is the projection of an idealization of the human heart's loftiest aspirations. But if these young men should some day come to accept the idea of God's existence, it will be this God and no other whom they will recognize. One expresses it thus:

If there is a true religion, the object of such a faith is not the type of vague god most Japanese have in mind, but the Christian God.

Another group, of about 30 percent of the respondents, equates God with nature. with nature's mysterious forces and energies, or with the fixed laws that govern all the visible world. Here is what one young man had to say on this subject:

As for me, I try to think of the so-called absolute being as the law of nature, the phenomenon of nature, the power of nature.

About 15 percent associate God with the spirits of ancestors; another 10 percent, approximately, connect God mainly with the pluralistic concept of the gods of mythology.

The majority view of the students, then, is that the human heart tries to evade thoughts of death, avoid what is fleeting and relative, and seeks indefatigably for what is absolute. It creates this absolute, this truth, this goodness, and this supreme beauty as the composite idealization of its aspirations and desires. This absolute being is a clear fabrication of man's imagination; it is the ideal for which he strives, and though it does not exist in reality, it can guide and inspire him.

The afterlife We conducted this survey among 109 university students from the Department of Economics and the Department of Law of Sophia University. The data show us that 70 percent clearly deny any belief in the afterlife; 9 percent believe in it fully; and 21 percent, allowing themselves to be carried away by their hearts' impulses without knowing exactly why, have a definite suspicion that death is not man's end but the beginning of another and better life that is eternal.

Interestingly, among numerous students the questions of the existence of God and of life after death are independent topics, totally dissociated from each other. Most noteworthy is the fact that only 6.4 percent answered affirmatively to the statements which present the afterlife as one of happiness and complete satisfaction of the most profound human ambitions and aspirations. In the same surprising manner, only 8.2 percent accepted the thesis that life hereafter is either a reward for the good or a just punishment for the bad, while 78.1 percent rejected it. The main explanation for these answers, as gleaned from various personal interviews conducted afterwards, is that the students feel that to think of life after death as an existence replete with happiness, or as a reward for good work or as a penalty for evil done, is but to make use of a psychological mechanism for obtaining false, soothing relief during times of suffering and trial in the present life; such a belief in their opinion, is only a childish solution to the problem of moral evil in this world.

Student: "Because we need more levelheadedness in today's complex society, it would be good if man attached more importance to religion."

Student: *"Rather than spew words about religion and the like, it seems it would be better to use your spare time some other way."*

SECOND STUDY
RELIGIOUS ATTITUDES OF
THE JAPANESE MAN IN THE STREET

We limited the study to the religious attitudes of the adult male population (salaried men, self-employed workers, and laborers) between the ages of twenty and forty residing in the large cities. As stated in the Introduction of this book, we consider these categories most relevant to a survey of current religious attitudes in Japan.

The adult male population between the ages of twenty and forty comprises 16,548,088 inhabitants according to the 1965 national census. Further, 9,266,744 are residents of the Tokyo-Osaka zone. Each day these young people are found straying farther and farther away from agricultural work, and the younger they are the greater their aversion to working in the fields. As expected, a great percentage is employed in manufacturing. There are 4,508,057 men between the ages of twenty and forty working in industry, particularly in turning out machinery, transportation equipment, electrical appliances, metals, iron, steel, and chemical products.

The Japanese census divides the working population into three categories: employees, self-employed workers, and unpaid family workers. This last group consists principally of agricultural workers. Of the 13,301,000 who work in the nonagricultural industries, 11,962,000 are employees, and 1,339,000 are self-employed workers. The great majority of the latter are in the retail trade and services industries.

Categories

Considering the working groups according to their respective occupations, it is interesting to note the extraordinary increase of clerical workers. From 2,800,259 in 1960 they have gone to 4,208,000 in

1965, an increase of about 54 percent. The astounding increase in the number of clerical workers in these last few years is a clear indication of the great proportion of Japanese who aspire to a life that they deem more secure and comfortable—that of the "salaried man." The salaried man belongs to the new middle class that has grown so rapidly in the cities of postwar Japan, replacing the old and fast-disappearing middle class composed of small, independent entrepreneurs and landlords, still designated as "self-employed workers." This new social class, the salaried man, is perhaps the most worthy of attention from sociologists interested in the structural upheavals in the Japanese family and society.

METHODS USED IN THIS SURVEY

In the study of religious attitudes, we have utilized the scale that we constructed and made use of in the survey with university groups. In the pilot tests we have been able to prove that many of the questions on this scale were also adaptable to the mentality of the new subjects of our proposed investigation. We chose questions that were far easier to understand and which would assure us of more reliable replies. In some questions, for the purpose of simplification, we rephrased the thought and avoided terminology that could be considered philosophical or academic. The same pilot tests have shown us that all the questions in our questionnaire were simple enough to cause laborers no difficulty and at the same time not improper for presentation even to those with a university education.

All questions referring to the existence of God, the life hereafter, and images or ideas about God are based mainly on studies that reveal in some way the principal religious beliefs and ideas of the Japanese with regard to these problems.

Concerning the field of religious practices, we have limited ourselves to those considered the most extensive and traditional throughout Japan and which to the present are being observed by a great majority of the Japanese. These include prayer or worship before the Buddhist or Shintoist home altars, the participation in festivals or pilgrimages to local and national shrines, and the carrying of *omamori* (a term that means protection or defense in the form of some sort of amulet or talisman against all kinds of evil).

The sampling for our investigation was selected from the great urban centers of the Tokyo-Yokohama and Osaka-Kobe areas, and following the "replicated sampling method" we chose 1,605 men, spread out in the fourteen cities of these regions. In June 1967 we sent questionnaires to these 1,605 men by ordinary mail. Within ten days we received 505 replies, or 31.4% of the total. On June 20 we began a house-to-house poll of the 1,100 subjects who did not reply.

In Table 3 below we illustrate the proportion of responses obtained from our universe.

Table 3: Persons Responding from Two Urban Areas

	Tokyo-Yokohama		*Osaka-Kobe*		*Total*	
	No.	*%*	*No.*	*%*	*No.*	*%*
Answers	814	78.9	489	85.9	1,303	81.2
No answer	104	10.0	37	6.5	140	8.7
Refused to answer	118	11.4	43	7.6	161	10.1
Whole sampling	1,036	100.0	659	100.0	1,605	100.0

Distribution by age and employment of the 1,303 respondents can be seen in Table 4 overleaf.

The survey results indicate that only 14 percent of the males between twenty and forty years of age believe in some religion; they total 182 of the 1,303 who responded to the questionnaires. Nevertheless we have come upon another group of 52 persons who, denying membership in any creed, confess to having personal religious beliefs in God's existence. This group, which constitutes 4 percent of the population, should be added to the aforementioned group of believers. The overall number of believers would then be 18 percent and that of nonbelievers, 82 percent.

Table 4: Ages and Occupations of Respondents

Age	Self-employed	Salaried	Laborers	Total
20-24	43	128	118	289
25-29	86	204	88	378
30-34	80	182	90	352
36-39	88	146	50	284
Total	297	660	346	1,303

The distribution of the 182 subjects according to the different religions can be seen in Table 5 on p. 62.

The Sōka Gakkai group: In our survey only 5.4 percent of the subjects, but 38.4 percent of all believers, belong to the Sōka Gakkai. There is a difference in membership between salaried men and laborers; the 5.4 percent decreases in the former group to 3.6 percent, and increases in the latter to 7.8 percent. Furthermore, if one were to consider only the salaried man with a university background, the percentage does not even reach 1 percent. This is similar to the findings we obtained in our study of the university group.

Among the Sōka Gakkai members, 97 percent answered that the *butsudan*, or Buddhist altar where they enshrine the *Gohonzon*, dominates their homes. Fifty-seven percent of these members bow daily in adoration and recite the *daimoku* before the *Gohonzon*; 23 percent do not say the prayer daily but frequently: 1 percent recite it only a few times a year. Only 4.3 percent admit that they do not practice any adoration or prayers; 8.6 percent did not answer the question. The 80 percent that is faithful to the essential practices of their religion is doubtless the highest among all religious groups.

A greater percentage of positive answers was expected to the question of whether or not our subjects go on pilgrimages to the temples of the Nichiren Shōshū sect, to which Sōka Gakkai belongs. Only 34 percent responded in the affirmative. It is probable that because of their busy life or for economic reasons, many are prevented from participating in such pilgrimages. And yet we believe that all those who fervently comply with their religious duties of paying homage to *Gohonzon* and reciting the *daimoku* are anxious to visit at least once the Taiseki Temple, which they consider the universal core of the earth.

The custom of carrying on one's person an *omamori* for protection from all harm is considered a superstitious one that is not recognized by the Nichiren Shōshū sect. Consequently it is not widely practiced by Sōka Gakkai members. However, about 14 percent confess to carrying such amulets.

If we proceed from religious practices to the study of religious attitudes we would have to state that here, too, of all the groups of religious believers, the Sōka Gakkai followers have the most positive attitudes, although there is always among them a small percentage that is easily swayed by the religious mentality that actually prevails in Japan. Approximately 90 percent affirm the importance of religion, the necessity for all men to think about it, the transcendental role that it plays in bringing peace and happiness to the universe, and its part in teaching every man how to follow the right way in life.

Table 5
Respondents by Categories and Religious Affiliation

	Self-employed 297	Salaried 660	Laborers 346	Total 1,303
Traditional Buddhists				
No sect*	2	0	4	4
Tendaishū	1	0	0	1
Shinshū	3	5	2	10
Shingonshū	2	0	6	8
Jōdoshū	1	4	2	7
Montōshū	1	0	1	2
Zenshū	0	3	3	6
Sōdōshū	4	6	2	12
Nichirenshū	6	5	3	14
Total	20(6.7%)	25(3.8%)	19(5.4%)	64(4.9%)
New Religionists				
Shintoist				
Tenrikyō	1	2	2	5
Ōmoto	0	1	0	1
Konkōkyō	1	1	0	2
Buddhist				
Reiyūkai	1	2	1	4
Risshōkōseikai	2	1	3	6
Myōdōkai	0	1	0	1
Itsukotsushū	0	1	0	1
Sōka Gakkai	19(6.4%)	24(3.6%)	27(7.8%)	70(5.4%)
Independent				
Sekaikyūsekkyō	1	0	0	1
P. L. Kyōdan	1	1	0	2
Seichō no ie	0	2	0	2
Tanshinkyō	1	0	0	1
Reihōkai	1	1	0	2
Total	28(9.5%)	37(5.6%)	33(9.5%)	98(7.5%)
Christians				
No sect*	2	7	2	11
Catholicism	0	2	1	3
Protestantism	1	4	1	6
Total	3(1.0%)	13(2.0%)	4(1.1%)	20(1.5%)
GRAND TOTAL	51(17.2%)	75(11.4%)	56(16.1%)	182(14.0%)

*None specified by respondents

Convinced of the social role which their religion performs in the world, Sōka Gakkai adherents promptly accept the obligation imposed upon them in joining the organization—that of working for the conversion of the greatest possible number of people.

In the light of their replies to the other questions, we can understand the attitude of these adherents regarding their belief that the Sōka Gakkai religion is the only true faith. It is very natural that, in view of the syncretism and tolerance common in Japan regarding everything pertaining to religion, the majority of Japanese agree with—or at least do not oppose—the thought that, although all religions differ one from another, they are basically all the same; consequently it does not matter whether a person belongs to one religion or the other. In our survey, the percentage of all samplings (including the believers) that oppose this thought is only 22 percent; but among Sōka Gakkai members, 81.4 percent are in opposition to it.

This same 81.4 percent also strongly reject other negative ideas about religion that are quite prevalent in Japan. To Sōka Gakkai members, religion is never opposed to science or to reason. Neither is it any form of escape from reality. Much less is it a mere "recourse to the gods in time of tribulation," as the popular Japanese adage claims.

Nevertheless the tendency prevalent among the young people to associate religion with lack of self-confidence is also common to some Sōka Gakkai members. Only 66 percent oppose this opinion—a figure quite far below the 81 percent we encountered in the replies to the preceding questions.

The same Sōka Gakkai also provides us with an example of a religion that practically prescinds completely from God. Only 15.7 percent believe that God is not a mere human fabrication but a true entity who

The believing group actually exists. Whether they affirm, deny, or doubt the existence of God, the concept or image they have of him is not at all different from the image held by the members of other religious groups or even by nonbelievers. Here, as elsewhere, we do not find any one God concept more noticeably predominant than others. God is frequently identified with the mythological heavenly and earthly gods, with the spirits of ancestors protecting their descendents, or even with the spirits of great men who are worshipped as God. God is also frequently conceived as the power of nature that surpasses the power of man. About 25 percent of the members of Sŏka Gakkai consider God as the one absolute deity who surpasses the power of both man and nature; but they consider this God as nothing more than a yearning in man's heart.

With respect to the beliefs about life after death we find the influence of the karma doctrine (belief in the reincarnation of souls) in some 50 percent of the responses, and in the other 50 percent a great variety of ideas, of confusion, or plain ignorance with respect to the problem of the life hereafter.

All this indicates one of the characteristics most frequently attributed to the new religions of Japan. Interest in metaphysical problems, in the transcendental problems of God, in problems of the soul and of eternal life, is completely secondary and of no importance compared to the interest in religion only as it is intimately related to the present life. Religion is above all something extremely concrete and practical, its principal value lying in its intramundane messianic promises to believers that benefits and advantages, material as well as psychological and spiritual, can be accumulated in this life.

At the end of the questionnaire we presented our subjects with some further questions to discover toward what religion, if any, they feel most sympathetic or most antipathetic. In the case of Sōka Gakkai members, the answer is clear; 87 percent give their own religion as the one for which they feel the greatest admiration. The rest (13 percent) did not answer. In the remaining religious groups the percentage of those who replied that the religion they profess is the one to which they feel most drawn is considerably lower than this 87 percent.

In general the number is very low of those who indicate antipathy for any religion; but in the case of the Sōka Gakkai group the percentage is 52.8 percent. It is significant that 33 percent reply that they feel antipathy (*kirai*) toward *all* religions, with the exception of their own. This reply is peculiar to them, and is not found even in the group of nonbelievers. The other 19.8 percent indicate as the object of their antipathy some concrete religions, especially Christianity, Risshōkōseikai, and Tenrikyō. The antipathy of Sōka Gakkai toward these three religions is well known, and their attacks against them are harsh; of late, though, these attacks have diminished somewhat because the leaders themselves have realized that such actions create a bad impression among the Japanese people.

Another trait of the members is the identification of their religious beliefs with the political ideas of the Kōmeitō; 92.8 percent state that they give their votes to this political party.

The traditional Buddhist group: Buddhists or Shintoist altars dominate the homes of 79 percent of the believers in traditional Buddhism. Before these altars some 21.6 percent offer daily prayer and reverence. In addition to the 21.6 percent, another 37.5 percent occasionally perform these religious acts *(tokidoki)*; but 40.9 percent replied that they rarely bow before altars. The percentage of believers who, within a given year, visit the Buddhist and Shintoist temples reaches as high as 71.6 percent. These pilgrimages are an element of tradition deeply rooted in Japanese life, and they have the power to survive all forms of crises within Buddhism or Shintoism.

The practice of carrying an *omamori* is still widespread today, even among the young generation; 54.6 percent admit to owning and carrying such *omamori*.

In many cases the religious attitudes of the Buddhist group evince some superficial beliefs, a great lack of conviction about one's own religion, insecurity and ignorance in connection with major issues, and apprehension over the most essential values of faith in general. Only some 50 percent oppose the idea that religion is a pure form of escape, a mere human recourse to seek the gods in time of tribulation, and something that would no doubt vanish in the light of scientific discoveries.

It is likewise interesting to observe that in a group that admits to profession of a religious faith, 25 percent state that they are not sure whether it is better or worse for religion to exist in this world, and 31 percent deny or doubt that it would be fitting for a man to give serious thought to the problem of religion at some time or another in his lifetime.

About 55 percent do not recognize religion as the light that enlightens man and orients him in his travel through life; nor do they believe that religion can contribute in any manner whatsoever to peace among mankind.

The only true value of religion that a great majority recognizes is its infusion of peace into the soul and its support to the human heart in moments of affliction or tribulation. With very few exceptions, they maintain that personal feeling is the one de-

ciding factor in the acceptance of any religious faith;
67.1 percent display a great tolerance in affirming, or
at least not opposing, the opinion that all forms of
religion, however at variance with one another they
may be, are basically and practically the same.

Regarding the existence of God and a life hereafter, we encounter the same confusion, insecurity,
and ignorance. Of the sixty-four subjects in our
group, only eight believe in God. The image or associ-
ation of ideas connected with the word "God"
follows the traditional polytheistic faith, or the vague
idea of nature with its laws and extraordinary powers.
A minority group, probably influenced by the Christian concept, professes the idea of God as the only
supreme and personal being who transcends man and
nature. But the majority believe that all these concepts of God are antiquated and primitive, and they
content themselves with the purely subjective idea of
a God created by man—a projection of the basic aspirations of the human heart. Those desires for happiness, for infinity, for eternal life, for all good
things—these are what we call God.

The beliefs in a life after death are also quite ambiguous. About 30 percent evince in their replies a
consistent negation of such beliefs. Around 40 percent display an attitude of doubt or plain ignorance,
while 15 percent indicate a firm belief in the existence of a future life. Another 15 percent is inclined
to believe in such a future life, though with reserva-
tions and doubts, and consequently their replies are
variant and inconsistent, depending on the nature of
the question. Many of them conceive the survival of
the human spirit according to the reincarnational
doctrine of karma.

To the question of whether or not they feel any
affinity for an existing religion and, if so, which one,

we find in their replies clear evidence that their religious practices and attitudes are founded more on tradition and custom than on personal conviction, much less on a commitment to their faith; 47 percent answer that they feel no religion, including their own, has any special attraction for them; 17.2 percent respond that they are attracted to Christianity, a religion quite distinct from the one they already profess. A mere 35.8 percent acknowledge the faith which they actually profess—Buddhism. (It will be recalled that in the case of Sōka Gakkai the percentage was 87 percent.)

The fact that a relatively large percentage feel a more keen sympathy for Christianity than for their own faith is interesting. It proves that the influence of Christianity in Japan is far greater then the actual number of baptized persons. As for the faith toward which they feel some antipathy, 42.2 percent indicated Sōka Gakkai; 6.2 percent mentioned the new religions; and 51.6 percent felt no aversion for any religion. Significantly, not one subject mentioned Christianity as the object of his antipathy.

The new-religions group: Discounting Sōka Gakkai members, the twenty-eight believers in the new religions represent 2.1 percent of our survey. No detailed analysis will be made of the results inasmuch as a sample of twenty-eight subjects cannot be considered statistically representative. We therefore will limit ourselves to indicating the general religious trends of this little group.

As far as their practices and attitudes are concerned, the group lies somewhere between Sōka Gakkai followers and traditional Buddhists. In their religious practices they do not attain the degree of fervor found in the Sōka Gakkai, but they surpass that of the Buddhists. In their attitudes about religion *The believing group* a majority display a frankly positive reaction. But in contrast to Sōka Gakkai members and more in consonance with the traditional Japanese mentality, more than half the subjects believe that most religions are practically the same, and affirm that it is sentiment, not reasoning, that decides the choice of one or another. The social values of faith as a factor in securing peace and order in the world and society are affirmed by only twelve subjects.

As for the problems of the existence and the concept of God, no clear idea emerges from this group, as in the groups previously surveyed. Nor is this group much preoccupied with beliefs in a future life.

There is a vast difference between the attitudes of the traditional Buddhists and the members of these new religions regarding the attachment and esteem they display for the respective faiths they profess. The majority of the members of the new religions select their own faith as the one for which they feel a strong attraction. As for the religions which they look upon with disfavor, sixteen admit some antipathy toward Sōka Gakkai. The rest display no hostility toward any religion.

The Christian group: Christianity is represented in our survey by twenty subjects, and on basic religious issues their answers reflect positive attitudes. Nevertheless, within this group there are seven subjects who believe that religion is necessary only for those lacking self-confidence. The existence of God is affirmed by only nine subjects; seven have doubts about the matter; and four deny God's existence. With regard to the concept of God, thirteen hold the Christian concept of one personal God; four consider God an idealization and projection of the heart's desire. Eight subjects subscribe to a life hereafter, and five deny it. The concept of the soul's survival according to the karma doctrine is held by only two subjects.

One special distinction of this group is that not one subject feels attracted to any other religion besides Christianity. As for the religion for which they feel some disfavor, six mentioned the Sōka Gakkai.

But we must note a special difficulty that arises upon analyzing this group. Only nine have expressly identified the Christian religion (Catholic or Protestant) to which they belong. The other eleven referred to Christianity in general. Are these latter subjects real Christians in the sense that they have studied Christian doctrine and were baptized? Or are they simply what we call "sympathizers of Christianity" because they have a vague idea of Christianity and feel attracted to it?

In almost all of the religious surveys undertaken in Japan, the percentage of Christians is always greater than the number of Christians who are actually baptized. In all of Japan the latter figure does not go beyond 0.7 percent, and yet in most surveys the percentage of Christians is at least double that figure and often reaches 3.0 percent. This is completely the contrary of other religions; the actual percentage of believers in other creeds is always much less than the percentage furnished by official statistics.

Those Japanese who proclaim themselves Christians without being Christians in reality usually have a quite superficial knowledge of Christian doctrine, and their religious practices are almost nil. Consequently their religious attitudes and dogmatic beliefs in God, in the life hereafter, and in the immortality of the soul all reflect the vagueness and doubt characteristic of any superficial, confused, and unsure knowledge.

Taking this fact into account, we are inclined to

think that the eleven subjects in our survey who *The believing group* vaguely profess Christianity as their faith belong to the group of "sympathizers of Christianity" and have no deep knowledge of Christian doctrine. None of their answers reflect the Christian faith at all.

Independent believers: Four percent of the subjects we interviewed believe in the existence of God, but they deny belonging to any particular faith. This group of fifty-two people is the same one that replied negatively to the statement, "God did not create man; man created God." They answered affirmatively to "God really exists regardless of whether a man believes in him or not." The great majority have a favorable attitude toward Christianity.

The attitudes of this group with respect to religion are very favorable. Nevertheless, in the three questions which decidedly reflect the atmosphere and religious mentality prevailing in Japan—that is, religion is necessary only to those who need outside support in their troubles; religion is determined by feeling and not by reason; all religions are basically the same—the percentage of answers that are in harmony with such a mentality is very great.

Regarding the concept of God, those who have displayed a preference for Christianity generally elect that of the Christian God—transcendental, one, and personal. Their beliefs in the existence of a life hereafter are proportionately more firm and consistent.

The term "negative" does not refer to a group of *Negative group* militant atheists who fight against religion. This kind of direct attack against religion is very rare in Japan. The term means instead the absolute indifference, tinged with a real contempt, toward anything related to religion. This negative group is composed of 288 subjects who represent 22.1 percent of the total sampling. (We must remember that among university students the negative group consisted of approximately 25 percent of the student population.)

What is the religious behavior and attitude of this group? The Japanese tradition of having Buddhist and Shintoist altars in their homes is so ingrained that even in this group 32.5 percent preserve this custom; but they say they have never bowed their heads in prayer before these home altars. A surprisingly high percentage, 57.6 percent, at one time or another participates in festivals and pilgrimages to temples. From their answers, we surmise that participation is due to some moral pressure or social obligation, or it may be that they participate not for the religious values but merely to enjoy themselves as one would enjoy some popular or traditional entertainment.

A relatively large number—27.1 percent—also carry about on their person the *omamori*. When asked what the carrying of such amulets signified to them, some subjects answered that they did not wear an *omamori* because they thought it was blessed with powers to ward off calamity or sickness, but rather because carrying it is a custom in which they find that they feel at ease (*kimochi ga raku ni naru*). This is a psychological phenomenon difficult to explain logically; but it is typical of many superstitions prevalent even among those who intellectually recognize it as superstition.

The basic attitude toward religion common to all the members of this group is their negative answer to the statement: "It would be better if religion were to continue to exist in the world." For them there is no conceivable reason for the need of religion. Other attitudes with respect to religion parallel this basic opinion. To them, religion and every religious belief are totally fictitious; it is a world of deceit far re-

moved from the modern and scientific world of today
and they see nothing in it of positive worth.

The existence of God is accepted only on a subjective plane: it depends on man's faith and judgment. If man believes in the existence of God, then God exists; if he does not believe, then God does not exist. That is the reason why they do not hesitate to affirm that it is man who creates God. For them God is nothing more than a yearning of man's heart.

The negative attitude toward the existence of a future life and the immortality of the soul concurs with their negative attitude toward the existence of God. Nevertheless belief in the transmigration of the soul as well as in communication with the spirits of ancestors were accepted by a minority that fluctuated between 5 and 9 percent.

Questioned as to whether or not they sympathized with any religion, 94.4 percent answered "none"; 4.5 percent named Christianity; while 1.1 percent preferred Buddhism. As for the question of which religion inspired the most aversion in them, 68 percent did not name a definite religion; 28.1 percent named the Sōka Gakkai, and the rest—3.9 percent—one of the new religions.

In the preceding pages we have investigated the
two groups which are at oppositve poles in regard to religious attitudes: the believers and the negative group. But the group most representative of the young generation belongs to neither of these and can aptly be called "the indifferents." We can say that about 60 percent of the young generation belongs to this group, irrespective of age or social position. Of the 1,303 subjects of our sampling, 781 form the group of indifferents.

This group's religious indifference is based chiefly

on a practical agnosticism and a consciously admitted ignorance. They do not feel concerned over the religious problem, at least to the extent that it stimulates them to a study of it. Religion and anything pertaining to it are considered by them as something apart from their lives and the problems that daily beset them. It is a world distinct from the one in which they live and for the moment at least they feel no need for religion.

The religious indifference of most is not extended to any religious practice, especially those traditional ones that have been transmitted from generation to generation. Thus 59.3 percent preserve the Buddhist and Shintoist altars in their homes, and 34.5 percent offer, from time to time, prayers before these altars. Originally, these practices were authentic acts of a religious cult; however, in Japan today, they have lost their exclusively devotional character and are being performed even by those who deny having a religious faith of any sort. In many recent religious surveys, subjects are usually asked the reason for their performance of such acts of reverence before their home altars. An absolute majority replies that it is through force of habit and because it is a way of remembering their ancestors. The remembrance of ancestors and the feeling of unity with tradition and history are sentiments strongly imbued in the Japanese soul; and the clearest manifestation of that spirit of reverence, gratitude, and historical continuity are these acts of adoration before the *butsudan* and the *kamidana* in which that memory is revered.

The popular custom of pilgrimages to Shintoist and Buddhist shrines holds some appeal for this group, too; 60.8 percent reply that they occasionally participate in pilgrimages to temples where local or national festivals are observed. As explained previously, such

pilgrimages do not necessarily bespeak religious faith
in the participants.

The other religious practice of carrying a protective
amulet is not unknown to this group either, for 43.1
percent admit that they carry an *omamori* on their
person.

From their religious practices we move on to their
attitudes, and here we immediately note a significant
difference between them and the negative group.
More than 75 percent of the indifferents do not give
affirmative replies to the opinions that imply a clear
contempt for religion, and in this sense their attitudes
cannot be said to be antireligious. On the other hand,
there is a great increase in positive answers to those
other statements which, to the Japanese mentality,
do not contain any element of disdain toward religion
since they merely express the idea that religion is
necessary only for those who feel they need to lean
upon some deity or for those whose sentiments and
mental attitudes lead them to faith.

In the questions where religion is analyzed in its
positive aspects and values, the replies of the indifferent group differ even more from those of the negative
group. None of these questions obtained more than
17 percent affirmative replies from the latter group,
and many of them had an even lower percentage.
With the indifferents, these answers usually oscillate
between the 30 and 70 percent mark.

This analysis leads us to conclude that religious
indifference does not necessarily indicate that this
group has a clearly negative attitude toward religion.
The indifference is due exclusively to ignorance and
to an inability to understand the relationship that
faith can have with their present lives. What they have
experienced and seen of religion, and the religious
concepts and atmosphere prevailing among Japanese

youth today—the atmosphere in which they themselves have been reared—cause them to assume this air of indifference when they are interrogated or when they are asked to express their opinions freely.

However, in many subjects of this group we find there is a kind of philosophy of life behind their religious indifference. Japanese culture attempts to achieve a unity of nature and man. Man feels akin to nature. Celebrated Japanese poets say that the aim of poetry is nothing more than to explain life and death to man through the medium of natural phenomena. To observe the blossoming and withering of flowers, and to witness the change of seasons in a year, are happenings which enable man to understand his fate. To struggle against nature is madness. The phrase "conquering nature," is typical of the West and implies a concept of nature which is inadmissible in Japanese culture. Man should not aspire to conquer nature but to follow it. "Live in perfect harmony with Nature and you will learn to enjoy her." Prosperity and adversity, richness and poverty, high social position and low standing are factors determined by nature. Every event is simply nature's unchanging development. Nature's way requires resignation, and to follow nature's way is to travel on the right road. In our dialogues with these young men, we have frequently discovered what we might call a spirit of religiousness toward nature and the fate to which she has assigned them, as well as a deep spirit of resignation— a contented resignation—and acceptance of that fate. They share the common aspirations of the modern society in which they live, and strive to attain the utmost economic and material well-being. But deep within they are still living in continuous submission to whatever destiny prepares for them.

This philosophy of life has been handed down to

the modern Japanese by ancestors who taught him to live in unison with that nature which they symbolized in the thorny rose: *bara ni wa toge ga aru* ("No rose without thorns"). That is man's life and that is nature's destiny. It is absurd to search for a rose without thorns, to long for happiness which does not and cannot exist, to seek consolation in beliefs of perfect happiness in the other life and in gods who are said to look after man. To accept nature and man as they are, to accept the destiny of death—that is the only reasonable thing to do. But while man lives he should seek for and enjoy the little pleasures which nature offers, those roses he finds in his path. After death, he will return to Mother Nature from whence he has come.

This entire philosophy of life is what is behind their religious indifference. It is not that they feel any aversion to religion, as the negative group does. It is that they have found in this philosophy of life the answers to their problems and, as a consequence, they have no use for faith. They do not deny that faith can console men; nor do they refute any of the religious values. But they themselves do not need such consolations or values. And it is obvious to them, as it is to the majority of the Japanese, that the religious problem is an exclusively psychological one and not one of objective truth or falsity. They are convinced that no one can ever recognize the truth or falsity of religious teaching; the only reason for admitting such religions is the psychological need of men. Whoever does not feel such need has no cause to admit them.

This group's religious indifference, therefore, does not instill in them an open hostility to religion. It only effects an unconcern for beliefs and practices which tell them nothing and which are not necessary in their daily lives. To associate such beliefs with pre-

Indifferent group sent problems would be to look for a comfort not needed by one who has already unquestioningly accepted nature and his fate.

The opinions of this group about the existence of God and of a life hereafter are very similar to the opinions of the negative group.

Finally we shall analyze the sympathies and antipathies which our subjects experience for different religions. About 67 percent declare that no religion has any special attraction for them; about 61 percent indicate that they likewise have no aversion for any religion. In those who display sympathy and antipathy we observe traits similar to those found in the groups previously analyzed. The two faiths that are always the most preferred are Christianity (15.7 percent) and traditional Buddhism (12.5 percent). The Sōka Gakkai emerges once more as the principal religion of disfavor. Of the 299 subjects who expressed an aversion for some religion, 245 specified Sōka Gakkai; 41 others spoke in general of the new religions, and almost always mention Sōka Gakkai, as well as the Risshōkōseikai, Seichō no ie, P. L. Kyōdan, and the more ancient Tenrikyō. Aside from the members who join these religions, very few Japanese feel attracted toward any of them.

INFLUENCE OF SOCIORELIGIOUS FACTORS Here we analyze the religious attitudes and practices of our subjects according to the class categories of salaried men, self-employed workers, and laborers. A detailed analysis of the results obtained from these three groups has led us to conclude that their religious attitudes and practices are basically uniform. Consequently we can say that differences in social position and functions are sociological factors which do not greatly influence the religious world of the Japanese. Some small differences do exist among these groups, however. In their religious beliefs we can detect a slight difference in the percentage of believers. The percentage among salaried men is the smallest of all—11.4 percent; but this difference does not surpass 5 or 6 percent with respect to the laborers (16.1 percent) and the self-employed workers (17.2 percent). With regard to the opinion that religion is useful and necessary only to those who lack self-confidence, a slight difference of about 6 percent may be noted among the salaried men. They are the ones who more often associate lack of self-confidence with religion. There also appears to be some difference in the concept or image they have of God. The salaried men have the least respect for the traditional Buddhist and Shintoist concepts. With reference to a faith which appeals to them, or which they dislike, it is significant that Christianity is the religion to which most (18.3 percent) are attracted. *Classes of employment*

In our survey group we have 268 subjects between the ages of twenty and twenty-four; 399 between twenty-five and twenty-nine; 342 between thirty and thirty-four; and 294 between thirty-five and thirty-nine. When we analyze the results obtained from each of these classes, we find a general tendency among the younger subjects to be somewhat more negative toward religion; conversely, it is in the class between ages thirty-five and thirty-nine that we encounter the most positive attitudes. *Age brackets*

Among the youths aged twenty to twenty-four, only 11.6 percent profess religious faith; in the thirty-five to thirty-nine age bracket, 17.3 percent. In regard to religious practices, the difference between the two groups exceeds 10 percent and sometimes reaches 20 percent. As for paying homage to ancestors at least a few times a year, 38 percent of the adults observe the tradition, while only 25.4 percent

Age brackets   of the younger ones do so. Visiting temples or joining pilgrimages is also more common in the older group— 69.7 percent as opposed to 49.6 percent among the younger men.

Curiously, the difference concerning belief in the existence of God or in a life after death is practically nil. Statistically, we are faced with a surprising fact. There is not even a 1 percent difference in results obtained from the four age brackets. Those who stoutly maintain that God is only a creation of man make up 62 percent.

One last fact worthy of note is that, among those who display some sympathy for Christianity, the younger ones stand out; they are represented by 19.4 percent. In the group between the ages of thirty-five and thirty-nine, only 11.6 percent admit such sympathy.

Political affiliations   Upon analyzing the religious attitudes of our subjects according to their political affiliations, we concluded that—with the exception of the Sōka Gakkai members, whose absolute majority pertains to the Kōmeitō and whose religious attitudes are the most positive among all groups—we cannot establish a definite correlation between this sociological factor and their religious mentality and behavior.

Cultural levels   As a criterion for determining cultural levels, the education received in schools and universities can be considered: 354 subjects have had no education higher than middle school; 547 finished high school; and 383 are junior-college or university graduates.

In the religious beliefs of these groups we note a slight difference. Those in the lower cultural level who profess a religious faith are around 17.2 percent; of those who finished high school, 15 percent; and university or junior-college graduates, 9.9 percent.

Similarly, in the groups with a lower culture the per- *Cultural levels*
centage of those who have a polytheistic idea of God
or of the gods identified with their ancestors, or with
persons of note idealized by the Japanese people, is
higher than that of the groups with a university background. In contrast, those who identify God with the
power of the laws of nature, or whose conception of
him is that of a unique and absolute being or the
idealization of all the aspirations of the human heart,
comprise a larger percentage in the group with a
junior-college or university education.

With respect to life after death, the traditional concept of the reincarnation of souls, the visitation of
ancestral spirits to their homes during the *obon*
festivals, the communication with the spirits of the
deceased, are all more easily affirmed by those who
have not gone beyond middle school.

Finally, another typical difference among these
groups may be discerned from the sympathy they feel
for Christianity. With the college-university group, 23
percent display this sympathy; this percentage is
exactly double that of the percentage in the middle
school group, and very much higher than the percentage of the high-school group.

We observe that the religious practices of prayer *Religious practices*
and the veneration of ancestors have a correlation
with positive and favorable attitudes toward religion.
When we examine the religious practices of visiting
temples, joining pilgrimages, and wearing *omamori* to
determine if these also indicate a correlation with religious beliefs and attitudes, the results obtained are
negative.

We divided our 1,303 subjects into two large
groups of 761 subjects who observe the practice of
visiting temples, and 542 who have discarded it. The

Religious practices differences in both groups in their attitudes toward religion and in their beliefs are minor and without statistical significance. The same can be said about the results obtained from those who do, and those who do not, carry on the practice of wearing *omamori*: we did not see any meaningful differences here.

This finding reveals once more that these religious practices, at least in the case of a large segment of the entire Japanese population, do not indicate an authentically religious sentiment; nor do they presuppose a religious faith, or serve as evidence for favorable attitudes to religion.

Student: "The attitude of 'looking to God for salvation' means to stop looking at reality and to give up all personal efforts."

Student: "I see a good number of believers dedicatedly carrying out a life of service and I consider them to be excellent people."

RÉSUMÉ
THE RELIGIOUS SENTIMENT
OF THE JAPANESE

The results we obtained from the survey and their consequent analysis could lead us to a false interpretation of the religious situation in Japan. We have found that 82 percent of our subjects deny having any religious belief and that an even greater percentage deny or doubt the existence of God, the immortality of the soul, and the existence of life after death.

Moreover, we have come to doubt the genuine religious sincerity of those who do confess a belief in some religion. Are we not dealing, in many cases, with a religious faith based solely on the customs and traditions of Japan, a faith which lacks any personal conviction? Is it not an intramundane faith aimed at the acquisition of material advantages in this present life? Or a religious faith considered solely as a means or instrument for satisfying the basic psychological necessities of the human heart, and hence something merely subjective and sentimental? We also get the impression of a certain primitivism in faith and religious attitudes. Those who profess some religious faith are unable to explain the content of those beliefs. To all this should be added the religious practices, some clearly superstitious, which continue to be observed in Japan by a very large sector of the population, including many who have no religious belief.

Judging by Western standards, we would deduce that the great majority of Japanese are irreligious and atheistic, and that the faith of those who do believe is childish and primitive. Yet this judgment is probably wrong because it is based on a Western criterion and a Western mentality.

RÉSUMÉ   The totality of Western culture and philosophy is penetrated by a clear dualism affecting both the world of realities and the world of concepts. The logical and discursive tendency of the Western mind has led it on a constant search for "clear and distinct ideas." This culture of "clear and distinct ideas" has in the course of centuries formed a dualistic mentality which conceives both the empirical and transcendental realities of the world in groups of opposed and irreducible pairs (e.g., God—man, absolute—relative, soul—body, sin—virtue, truth—falsehood, etc.). All these distinctions, which so satisfy the logical curiosity of the Western intellect, lead to yet another and more profound dualism. On a higher level we encounter the realities of God, the absolute, the spirit, the human soul, truth, virtue, eternal life. On a lower level stands the world of creatures, matter, the body, contingency, the temporal, untruth, sin, death—all the realities that belong exclusively to this present world.

The man who consciously or unconsciously accepts this dualism will naturally develop certain attitudes toward each of these two worlds that will never be found in the man who denies it. This means that in this dualist conception it is easy to explain the attitude of the man who recognizes only the lower level of world empirical realities and denies the higher level of transcendental realities. In other words, an atheistic and materialistic mentality and attitude is possible—God can be clearly denied because he is clearly distinguishable from man and nature, the soul can be clearly denied because it is clearly distinguishable from the body, and so on.

The Japanese mentality is radically opposed to that of Western man. Could we not say that the Japanese feels antagonistic toward anything that is presented to him as perfectly "clear and distinct"? He has an innate dislike for defining things, an activity that his Western counterpart so enjoys. "The Japanese avoids all clear ideas, definitions, categories in his direct knowledge of things."* Certainly we do not find in all the thought and culture of Japan, at least in times prior to the influence of the West, any definitions of God, spirit, or the soul; of truth and falsehood; of sin and virtue; of good and evil; of sacred and profane.

Not only are these definitions nonexistent, but in practical life these two worlds, so clearly defined in traditional Western culture, are indistinguishable. If we imagine these two worlds as parallel lines then, when we attempt to analyze them in the culture of Japan, we will be obliged to treat them as one so that distinctions remain blurred. In explaining this monism to us, Japanese authors state that the essential difference between Western man and the Japanese lies in the fact that the former always raises in himself the question "this *or* that"? (*are ka kore ka*), whereas the Japanese fails to understand the meaning of such a dualism and will always repeat to himself "this and that too" (*are mo kore mo*).

In this absolute monism, what sense can there be in denying God, the spirits, the soul—in short, in denying religion?

The Japanese denies religion—that is, all the concrete religions which exist in the world—because he has never considered any religion as such an absolute, nor has he ever considered any religious belief an immutable truth. He has never accepted religions for

---

*Karaki Junzoo, "Shizen to iu koto," ed. Kamei Katsuichiroo and Usui Yoshimi, *Nihon no bi,* p. 93.

their content, but rather for their "form." In Japanese culture religions are conceived as "ways" or "manners" of life which are in no way absolute and which all more or less lead to the same goal. The doctrinal content is entirely secondary. For the Japanese the most essential thing is his interior attitude, a blend of intuition and affectivity, in which his own self is developed to the exclusion of any clearly formulated ideology. Faith and religious practices are considered means by which the human heart is strengthened. Religion is something relative created by man.

Precisely one of the reasons for not distinguishing the two worlds envisioned in the dualistic conception of Western man is that it is, after all, man himself who creates religions. It is man himself who thinks and imagines God and gods, who speaks to us of the transmigration of the souls, or of heaven and hell. It is man who affirms that this constitutes sin and that a virtue. Hence all this is totally relative because it issues from man who is himself essentially relative.

There are probably very few people in the world other than the Japanese who have savored more deeply the taste of contingency, (the *mujoo*, the *hakanasa*, or the *munashisa*) that pervades all created things. In the depth with which the Japanese experiences the loneliness and alienation of man (the *sabishisa, kodoku, sogai*) can be found the principal reason why he regards all things as relative. And in that interrelationship and relativism are included religions and gods and all other teachings transmitted by man. They all remain on the level of things worldly and human, along that single horizontal line acknowledged by the Japanese.

And yet, paradoxical though it may seem, such an

attitude of mind produces an inclination for the religious which enables us to affirm that the Japanese soul possesses a deep religious sentiment. For as the Japanese advances in years, he senses more and more the emptiness of things; then, without any reasoning, with no logical arguments of any kind, and guided solely by his extraordinarily developed powers of intuition, and his sensitivity, he consciously or subconsciously attempts to cross the barrier of all that is relative in order to reach the "something" which cannot be expressed because as soon as it is expressed it ceases to be this "something."

It is Nishitani Keiji who, in his profound essay on "The Religious Conscience in Japanese Tradition"* succeeds best in explaining the meaning of that "something" (*nanika*) and the attitude that the Japanese have toward it. He states that the quintessence of the Japanese spirit consists in the reaching out "to touch, to contact experientially the reality of things." It consists in "the immediate perception of authentic reality"; in the ability "to touch, to sense the authentic reality of things in their bare ontological reality, transcending every intellectual concept and discourse," and "to penetrate to the deepest recesses of the original source of being." But the author has no words with which to explain what that ultimate ontological reality is, since it is impossible to express it in words. The only thing he says is that it is "something totally different." Religion is "this intuitive-affective contemplation of that authentic reality."

The Japanese, in his constant search for that

---

*In Takeda Kiyo, ed., *Shisooshi no hoohoo to taishoo,* pp. 241-271.

"something" looks at himself, at things, and at nature with special eyes; and his intuitive heart leads him to discover in that affective contemplation of nature and in his phenomenological experience of daily events what in the West would be termed "divine" aspects or elements—*shinteki na mono*, as Nishitani Keiji calls them. They are experiences which transcend all other phenomenogical experiences.

What conclusions can be drawn from all that has been said until now? First of all we must point out that the word "atheist" cannot be applied with the same meaning to both the Western and the Japanese people. Unlike the Western atheist, who denies all transcendental beliefs, many nonbelieving Japanese will not deny the existence of that "something" which they cannot express and which no one can explain to them. It is something that only he himself can discover, and it is a search without end, one that is never satisfied. Professor Anzai calls the Japanese a perpetual *kyuudoosha*, a permanent "catechumen," in his search for the absolute, for that "authentic original existence" which, in the opinion of the well-known Japanese Protestant, Nitobi Inazoo, needs only to be given the name *You* to become the personal Christian God.

In giving this explanation we in no way wish to make the reader believe that this search takes place in every Japanese. Moreover, we are inclined to think, as do many others, that the Japanese—growing more and more Westernized in his ways, and more and more materialistic in his daily life—is losing the powers of intuition and contemplation that he formerly possessed. But we do maintain that in many who seem to be nonbelievers and nihilists there exists this deep religious sentiment which makes them receptive to the world of the absolute, the sacred, the immutable, the eternal.

Secondly, we think it would be a mistake to use as a criterion for judging the religious spirit of the Japanese their affiliation or nonaffiliation with some particular religion. All their religions and religious practices, and their sometimes total and unconditional commitment to the religious group to which they belong, are for the Japanese merely phenomenological and contingent realities—intramundane, relative, and changeable realities which are accepted because as they provide material, psychological, or spiritual support for their lives. He will reject these as soon as he ceases to receive from them personal gains. The only difference between the believer and nonbeliever in Japan is that the former admits a set of empirical, relative, intramundane values which satisfy him personally, but which, for the nonbeliever, has no meaning. In the nonbeliever, on the other hand, we may find that same deep religious sentiment consisting in an openness to the divine and to the absolute, to the authentic source of all existence. This attitude, the only one that constitutes the true religious spirit of the Japanese, can be found in both believer and nonbeliever; it may also be lacking in both. In Japan, the criterion of "believer" and "nonbeliever" does not suffice to make an adequate distinction between those souls that are truly religious and those that are irreligious or indifferent.

Thirdly, we would like to say that it will be very difficult for the Japanese to accept any particular religion, even more so if that religion presents him with a "prefabricated God" and one that is "foreign" to him and to his personal experience. In this sense, the traditonal way of presenting the God of Christianity

RÉSUMÉ as the rational conclusion of a few logical arguments, with no existential relationship to man, lacks meaning in the Oriental psychology. As the Japanese authors Kobayashi Kooichi and Miura Masashi say, in order to awaken in the Japanese a religious sentiment that will enable him to attain God, it is necessary that "every Japanese start by fixing his eyes on himself, by confronting himself, and by reaching down to the deepest recesses of his own personal existence."*

Nihonjin no nihiru to mu, p. 206.

Picture Credits

Graham McDonnell, M.M.: cover, half title, pp. 2, 7, 9, 47, 49, 55, 56, 57, 83, 85, and this page. James P. Colligan, M.M.: pp. 1, 8, 84. Lawrence O'Neill: cover, p. 3. Kazuko Tange: cover.

The photographers whose works are credited above are not roving photojournalists but men who have lived and worked in Japan. Like the students' comments throughout the First Study these pictures may help readers to "contact experientially" the realities that the author analyzes.